KETO DIET

D1609042

Weight Tracker

Want a freebie?
Email us at lovelybluebook@gmail.com
Our website:
www.bluebookpress.com

Introduction to The Keto Diet

Ketogenic Diet

The keto diet is a strict low carb diet that requires you to dramatically decrease your carb intake. This could mean consuming anywhere from 20-50 grams of carbs per day depending on your gender, weight, and activity level.

Limiting your diet to low carb foods and healthy fats leads your body into ketosis which is a metabolic state in which your body burns fat stores for energy rather than glucose.

The Ketogenic Diet Keeps You full for a long time. The high level of healthy fat in the keto diet also makes it much easier to stay full –bellied in a fasted state and eliminates those intense feelings of hunger and cravings throughout the day that are usually the greatest obstacles when trying to lose weight.

You avoid all sugary as well as processed foods on a **ketogenic diet**. Some vegetables and fruits also need to be avoided because of the number of carbs they contain.

Vegetables to avoid on keto: Potatoes, carrots, peas, beets, parsnips, sweet potato, butternut squash, most beans, corn, beets, yams.

Fruits to avoid on keto: Bananas, Mangos, Pears, Apples, Pineapples, Plumps, Dates, Grapes, Oranges, Pomegranates, Nectarines, Peaches, Melons, Tangerines, Figs, Kiwi, Prunes.

Benefits

- Weight Loss
- Appetite Suppressant - You're in more control of your hunger when your body turns to fat stores for energy making Intermittent Fasting easier.
- Type 2 Diabetes Improvements
- Healthy Heart Benefits: Many studies show improved cholesterol figures, lowered blood pressure and, a more balanced heart rate
- Better Focus/Clarity/Understanding

KETO FOOD PYRAMID

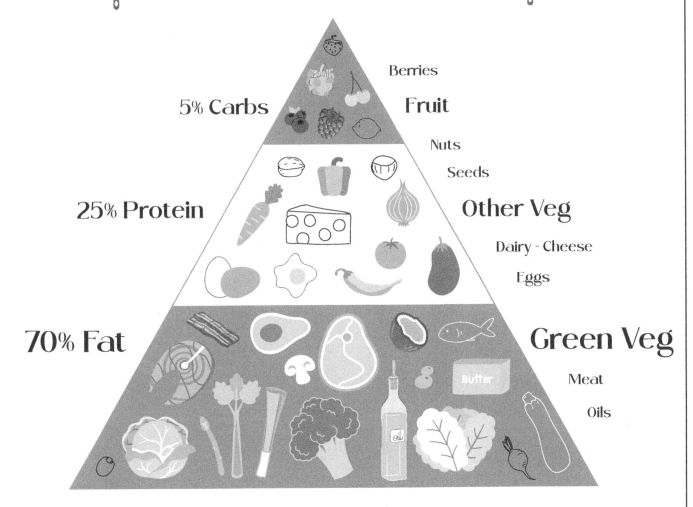

5% Carbs — Berries, Fruit

25% Protein — Nuts, Seeds, Other Veg, Dairy - Cheese, Eggs

70% Fat — Green Veg, Meat, Oils

DON'T EAT:

KETO DIET SHOPPING LIST:

Vegetables

Leafy greens: Arugula,
Spinach, Kale, Cabbage
Lettuce
Leeks
Celery
Cucumber
Broccoli
Cauliflower
Brussels sprouts
Asparagus
Zucchini
Bell peppers
Mushrooms
Onions
Squashes
Radishes
Eggplant

Protein

Chicken
Turkey } pasture-raised poultry
Duck
Beef
Pork } grass-fed
Lamb
Venison
Salmon
Tuna
Shrimp } wild-caught
Crab   Seafood
Anchovies
Eggs

Oils

Olive oil
Coconut oil
Nut oils
MCT oil

Dairy

Hard cheeses
Cottage cheese
Greek yogurt
Butter
Ghee
Heavy cream

**AVOID ALL PROCESSED FOOD AND STICK TO WHOLE NATURAL FOODS
WHENEVER POSSIBLE LIMIT CARBS INTAKE TO UNDER 20G PER DAY
TO KEEP YOU IN KETOSIS AND FAT BURNING MODE!**

KETO DIET SHOPPING LIST:

Nuts & Seeds

Walnuts
Pecans
Almonds
Macadamia nuts
Brazil nuts
Flaxseed
Chia seeds
Sesame seeds
Sunflower Seeds
Pumpkin Seeds
Pistachios

Fruits

Blackberries
Raspberries
Blueberries
Strawberries
Lemons
Limes
Tomatoes
Avocado
Olives

Beverages

Coffee
Tea
Still water
Sparkling water

FOOD TO AVOID ON KETO:

SUGAR: fruit smoothies and juices, apples, bananas, lychees, figs, mango, grapes, pears, syrup, candy, soda (include diet soda), honey, artificial sweeteners, cookies, ice-cream, pastries

STARCHES AND GRAINS: oats, potatoes, beans (black beans, pinto, lima, chickpeas, lentils), yams, corn, flour, rice, pasta, bread, pizza, bagels, waffles, pancakes, french fries, cereal, muffins, crackers, chips

ALCOHOL. MILK. VEGETABLE OIL. DRIED FRUIT. LOW-FAT PRODUCTS

Tips to Get Started:

- Have healthy meals during your eating window - the best keto-friendly foods - (max-20 g carbs)

- Eat fatty, satisfying meals. Eating fatty foods will make it a lot easier and sustainable. Keto foods are healthy and make you full, so you won't be hungry during your meals.

- Eat Enough: During your eating windows be sure you are eating enough and you feel full.

- For the first two weeks, you should do light exercise, without overstraining until you know how your body reacts to Ketosis.

- Stay hydrated make sure you are drinking enough fluids (water) to avoid dehydration!

The Keto diet is a safe and powerful tool for improving your health as well as increasing

your activity levels. If you want to use fasting for ketosis, it's ideal if you do it while following a keto diet.

You will achieve stunning results!

NOTES

DATA:		KETO DIET			

	FATS	PROTEIN	CARBS	NUMBER OF MEALS	
MON					SUGAR ◯ YES ◯ NO
					COFFEE ◯ YES ◯ NO
					WATER ◯ YES ◯ NO
					WORKOUT ◯ YES ◯ NO

	FATS	PROTEIN	CARBS	NUMBER OF MEALS	
TUE					SUGAR ◯ YES ◯ NO
					COFFEE ◯ YES ◯ NO
					WATER ◯ YES ◯ NO
					WORKOUT ◯ YES ◯ NO

	FATS	PROTEIN	CARBS	NUMBER OF MEALS	
WED					SUGAR ◯ YES ◯ NO
					COFFEE ◯ YES ◯ NO
					WATER ◯ YES ◯ NO
					WORKOUT ◯ YES ◯ NO

	FATS	PROTEIN	CARBS	NUMBER OF MEALS	
THU					SUGAR ◯ YES ◯ NO
					COFFEE ◯ YES ◯ NO
					WATER ◯ YES ◯ NO
					WORKOUT ◯ YES ◯ NO

	FATS	PROTEIN	CARBS	NUMBER OF MEALS	
FRI					SUGAR ◯ YES ◯ NO
					COFFEE ◯ YES ◯ NO
					WATER ◯ YES ◯ NO
					WORKOUT ◯ YES ◯ NO

NOTES & ACCOMPLISHMENT

DATA: _____	KETO DIET

	FATS	PROTEIN	CARBS	NUMBER OF MEALS	SUGAR ◯ YES ◯ NO
SAT					COFFEE ◯ YES ◯ NO
					WATER ◯ YES ◯ NO
					WORKOUT ◯ YES ◯ NO

	FATS	PROTEIN	CARBS	NUMBER OF MEALS	SUGAR ◯ YES ◯ NO
SUN					COFFEE ◯ YES ◯ NO
					WATER ◯ YES ◯ NO
					WORKOUT ◯ YES ◯ NO

ENERGY LEVEL

SUN	MON	TUE	WED	THU	FRI	SAT

OBSERVATIONS - HOW I FEEL

MY GOAL THIS WEEK

MEASUREMENT:

WEIGHT:

CHEST.............................WAIST...............................HIPS...............................

DATA:		KETO DIET				

	FATS	PROTEIN	CARBS	NUMBER OF MEALS	SUGAR ◯ YES ◯ NO
MON					COFFEE ◯ YES ◯ NO
					WATER ◯ YES ◯ NO
					WORKOUT ◯ YES ◯ NO

	FATS	PROTEIN	CARBS	NUMBER OF MEALS	SUGAR ◯ YES ◯ NO
TUE					COFFEE ◯ YES ◯ NO
					WATER ◯ YES ◯ NO
					WORKOUT ◯ YES ◯ NO

	FATS	PROTEIN	CARBS	NUMBER OF MEALS	SUGAR ◯ YES ◯ NO
WED					COFFEE ◯ YES ◯ NO
					WATER ◯ YES ◯ NO
					WORKOUT ◯ YES ◯ NO

	FATS	PROTEIN	CARBS	NUMBER OF MEALS	SUGAR ◯ YES ◯ NO
THU					COFFEE ◯ YES ◯ NO
					WATER ◯ YES ◯ NO
					WORKOUT ◯ YES ◯ NO

	FATS	PROTEIN	CARBS	NUMBER OF MEALS	SUGAR ◯ YES ◯ NO
FRI					COFFEE ◯ YES ◯ NO
					WATER ◯ YES ◯ NO
					WORKOUT ◯ YES ◯ NO

NOTES & ACCOMPLISHMENT

DATA: _____	**KETO DIET**				

SAT	FATS	PROTEIN	CARBS	NUMBER OF MEALS	SUGAR ○ YES ○ NO
					COFFEE ○ YES ○ NO
					WATER ○ YES ○ NO
					WORKOUT ○ YES ○ NO

SUN	FATS	PROTEIN	CARBS	NUMBER OF MEALS	SUGAR ○ YES ○ NO
					COFFEE ○ YES ○ NO
					WATER ○ YES ○ NO
					WORKOUT ○ YES ○ NO

ENERGY LEVEL

SUN	MON	TUE	WED	THU	FRI	SAT

OBSERVATIONS - HOW I FEEL

MY GOAL THIS WEEK

MEASUREMENT:

WEIGHT:

CHEST................................WAIST................................HIPS................................

DATA:		**KETO DIET**			

MON	FATS	PROTEIN	CARBS	NUMBER OF MEALS	SUGAR ○ YES ○ NO
					COFFEE ○ YES ○ NO
					WATER ○ YES ○ NO
					WORKOUT ○ YES ○ NO

TUE	FATS	PROTEIN	CARBS	NUMBER OF MEALS	SUGAR ○ YES ○ NO
					COFFEE ○ YES ○ NO
					WATER ○ YES ○ NO
					WORKOUT ○ YES ○ NO

WED	FATS	PROTEIN	CARBS	NUMBER OF MEALS	SUGAR ○ YES ○ NO
					COFFEE ○ YES ○ NO
					WATER ○ YES ○ NO
					WORKOUT ○ YES ○ NO

THU	FATS	PROTEIN	CARBS	NUMBER OF MEALS	SUGAR ○ YES ○ NO
					COFFEE ○ YES ○ NO
					WATER ○ YES ○ NO
					WORKOUT ○ YES ○ NO

FRI	FATS	PROTEIN	CARBS	NUMBER OF MEALS	SUGAR ○ YES ○ NO
					COFFEE ○ YES ○ NO
					WATER ○ YES ○ NO
					WORKOUT ○ YES ○ NO

NOTES & ACCOMPLISHMENT

DATA: _____	KETO DIET

	FATS	PROTEIN	CARBS	NUMBER OF MEALS		
SAT					SUGAR ◯ YES ◯ NO	
					COFFEE ◯ YES ◯ NO	
					WATER ◯ YES ◯ NO	
					WORKOUT ◯ YES ◯ NO	

	FATS	PROTEIN	CARBS	NUMBER OF MEALS		
SUN					SUGAR ◯ YES ◯ NO	
					COFFEE ◯ YES ◯ NO	
					WATER ◯ YES ◯ NO	
					WORKOUT ◯ YES ◯ NO	

ENERGY LEVEL

SUN	MON	TUE	WED	THU	FRI	SAT

OBSERVATIONS - HOW I FEEL

MY GOAL THIS WEEK

MEASUREMENT:

CHEST.................................WAIST.................................HIPS.................................

WEIGHT:

DATA:		KETO DIET				

MON

FATS	PROTEIN	CARBS	NUMBER OF MEALS	SUGAR ◯ YES ◯ NO
				COFFEE ◯ YES ◯ NO
				WATER ◯ YES ◯ NO
				WORKOUT ◯ YES ◯ NO

TUE

FATS	PROTEIN	CARBS	NUMBER OF MEALS	SUGAR ◯ YES ◯ NO
				COFFEE ◯ YES ◯ NO
				WATER ◯ YES ◯ NO
				WORKOUT ◯ YES ◯ NO

WED

FATS	PROTEIN	CARBS	NUMBER OF MEALS	SUGAR ◯ YES ◯ NO
				COFFEE ◯ YES ◯ NO
				WATER ◯ YES ◯ NO
				WORKOUT ◯ YES ◯ NO

THU

FATS	PROTEIN	CARBS	NUMBER OF MEALS	SUGAR ◯ YES ◯ NO
				COFFEE ◯ YES ◯ NO
				WATER ◯ YES ◯ NO
				WORKOUT ◯ YES ◯ NO

FRI

FATS	PROTEIN	CARBS	NUMBER OF MEALS	SUGAR ◯ YES ◯ NO
				COFFEE ◯ YES ◯ NO
				WATER ◯ YES ◯ NO
				WORKOUT ◯ YES ◯ NO

NOTES & ACCOMPLISHMENT

DATA: [_____] **KETO DIET**

SAT

	FATS	PROTEIN	CARBS	NUMBER OF MEALS		
					SUGAR	◯YES ◯NO
					COFFEE	◯YES ◯NO
					WATER	◯YES ◯NO
					WORKOUT	◯YES ◯NO

SUN

	FATS	PROTEIN	CARBS	NUMBER OF MEALS		
					SUGAR	◯YES ◯NO
					COFFEE	◯YES ◯NO
					WATER	◯YES ◯NO
					WORKOUT	◯YES ◯NO

ENERGY LEVEL

😄 🙂 😏 😮 😖 😵

SUN	MON	TUE	WED	THU	FRI	SAT

OBSERVATIONS - HOW I FEEL

MY GOAL THIS WEEK

MEASUREMENT:

WEIGHT:

CHEST.................................WAIST.................................HIPS.................................

DATA:		KETO DIET				

	FATS	PROTEIN	CARBS	NUMBER OF MEALS		
MON					SUGAR ◯ YES ◯ NO	
					COFFEE ◯ YES ◯ NO	
					WATER ◯ YES ◯ NO	
					WORKOUT ◯ YES ◯ NO	

	FATS	PROTEIN	CARBS	NUMBER OF MEALS		
TUE					SUGAR ◯ YES ◯ NO	
					COFFEE ◯ YES ◯ NO	
					WATER ◯ YES ◯ NO	
					WORKOUT ◯ YES ◯ NO	

	FATS	PROTEIN	CARBS	NUMBER OF MEALS		
WED					SUGAR ◯ YES ◯ NO	
					COFFEE ◯ YES ◯ NO	
					WATER ◯ YES ◯ NO	
					WORKOUT ◯ YES ◯ NO	

	FATS	PROTEIN	CARBS	NUMBER OF MEALS		
THU					SUGAR ◯ YES ◯ NO	
					COFFEE ◯ YES ◯ NO	
					WATER ◯ YES ◯ NO	
					WORKOUT ◯ YES ◯ NO	

	FATS	PROTEIN	CARBS	NUMBER OF MEALS		
FRI					SUGAR ◯ YES ◯ NO	
					COFFEE ◯ YES ◯ NO	
					WATER ◯ YES ◯ NO	
					WORKOUT ◯ YES ◯ NO	

NOTES & ACCOMPLISHMENT

SAT	FATS	PROTEIN	CARBS	NUMBER OF MEALS	SUGAR ◯ YES ◯ NO
					COFFEE ◯ YES ◯ NO
					WATER ◯ YES ◯ NO
					WORKOUT ◯ YES ◯ NO

SUN	FATS	PROTEIN	CARBS	NUMBER OF MEALS	SUGAR ◯ YES ◯ NO
					COFFEE ◯ YES ◯ NO
					WATER ◯ YES ◯ NO
					WORKOUT ◯ YES ◯ NO

ENERGY LEVEL

SUN	MON	TUE	WED	THU	FRI	SAT

OBSERVATIONS - HOW I FEEL

MY GOAL THIS WEEK

MEASUREMENT:

WEIGHT:

CHEST............................WAIST............................HIPS............................

DATA:		KETO DIET					

MON	FATS	PROTEIN	CARBS	NUMBER OF MEALS	SUGAR ◯ YES ◯ NO
					COFFEE ◯ YES ◯ NO
					WATER ◯ YES ◯ NO
					WORKOUT ◯ YES ◯ NO

TUE	FATS	PROTEIN	CARBS	NUMBER OF MEALS	SUGAR ◯ YES ◯ NO
					COFFEE ◯ YES ◯ NO
					WATER ◯ YES ◯ NO
					WORKOUT ◯ YES ◯ NO

WED	FATS	PROTEIN	CARBS	NUMBER OF MEALS	SUGAR ◯ YES ◯ NO
					COFFEE ◯ YES ◯ NO
					WATER ◯ YES ◯ NO
					WORKOUT ◯ YES ◯ NO

THU	FATS	PROTEIN	CARBS	NUMBER OF MEALS	SUGAR ◯ YES ◯ NO
					COFFEE ◯ YES ◯ NO
					WATER ◯ YES ◯ NO
					WORKOUT ◯ YES ◯ NO

FRI	FATS	PROTEIN	CARBS	NUMBER OF MEALS	SUGAR ◯ YES ◯ NO
					COFFEE ◯ YES ◯ NO
					WATER ◯ YES ◯ NO
					WORKOUT ◯ YES ◯ NO

NOTES & ACCOMPLISHMENT

DATA:		KETO DIET			

SAT	FATS	PROTEIN	CARBS	NUMBER OF MEALS	SUGAR ◯ YES ◯ NO
					COFFEE ◯ YES ◯ NO
					WATER ◯ YES ◯ NO
					WORKOUT ◯ YES ◯ NO

SUN	FATS	PROTEIN	CARBS	NUMBER OF MEALS	SUGAR ◯ YES ◯ NO
					COFFEE ◯ YES ◯ NO
					WATER ◯ YES ◯ NO
					WORKOUT ◯ YES ◯ NO

ENERGY LEVEL

SUN	MON	TUE	WED	THU	FRI	SAT

OBSERVATIONS - HOW I FEEL

MY GOAL THIS WEEK

MEASUREMENT:

WEIGHT:

CHEST..................................WAIST..................................HIPS..................................

DATA:		KETO DIET				

MON

FATS	PROTEIN	CARBS	NUMBER OF MEALS	SUGAR ○YES ○NO
				COFFEE ○YES ○NO
				WATER ○YES ○NO
				WORKOUT ○YES ○NO

TUE

FATS	PROTEIN	CARBS	NUMBER OF MEALS	SUGAR ○YES ○NO
				COFFEE ○YES ○NO
				WATER ○YES ○NO
				WORKOUT ○YES ○NO

WED

FATS	PROTEIN	CARBS	NUMBER OF MEALS	SUGAR ○YES ○NO
				COFFEE ○YES ○NO
				WATER ○YES ○NO
				WORKOUT ○YES ○NO

THU

FATS	PROTEIN	CARBS	NUMBER OF MEALS	SUGAR ○YES ○NO
				COFFEE ○YES ○NO
				WATER ○YES ○NO
				WORKOUT ○YES ○NO

FRI

FATS	PROTEIN	CARBS	NUMBER OF MEALS	SUGAR ○YES ○NO
				COFFEE ○YES ○NO
				WATER ○YES ○NO
				WORKOUT ○YES ○NO

NOTES & ACCOMPLISHMENT

DATA:		KETO DIET					

	FATS	PROTEIN	CARBS	NUMBER OF MEALS	SUGAR ◯ YES ◯ NO
SAT					COFFEE ◯ YES ◯ NO
					WATER ◯ YES ◯ NO
					WORKOUT ◯ YES ◯ NO

	FATS	PROTEIN	CARBS	NUMBER OF MEALS	SUGAR ◯ YES ◯ NO
SUN					COFFEE ◯ YES ◯ NO
					WATER ◯ YES ◯ NO
					WORKOUT ◯ YES ◯ NO

ENERGY LEVEL

SUN	MON	TUE	WED	THU	FRI	SAT

OBSERVATIONS - HOW I FEEL

MY GOAL THIS WEEK

MEASUREMENT:

WEIGHT:

CHEST................................WAIST................................HIPS................................

DATA:		KETO DIET				

MON

FATS	PROTEIN	CARBS	NUMBER OF MEALS		
				SUGAR ⭘YES ⭘NO
				COFFEE ⭘YES ⭘NO
				WATER ⭘YES ⭘NO
				WORKOUT ⭘YES ⭘NO

TUE

FATS	PROTEIN	CARBS	NUMBER OF MEALS		
				SUGAR ⭘YES ⭘NO
				COFFEE ⭘YES ⭘NO
				WATER ⭘YES ⭘NO
				WORKOUT ⭘YES ⭘NO

WED

FATS	PROTEIN	CARBS	NUMBER OF MEALS		
				SUGAR ⭘YES ⭘NO
				COFFEE ⭘YES ⭘NO
				WATER ⭘YES ⭘NO
				WORKOUT ⭘YES ⭘NO

THU

FATS	PROTEIN	CARBS	NUMBER OF MEALS		
				SUGAR ⭘YES ⭘NO
				COFFEE ⭘YES ⭘NO
				WATER ⭘YES ⭘NO
				WORKOUT ⭘YES ⭘NO

FRI

FATS	PROTEIN	CARBS	NUMBER OF MEALS		
				SUGAR ⭘YES ⭘NO
				COFFEE ⭘YES ⭘NO
				WATER ⭘YES ⭘NO
				WORKOUT ⭘YES ⭘NO

NOTES & ACCOMPLISHMENT

DATA: _____   **KETO DIET**

SAT	FATS	PROTEIN	CARBS	NUMBER OF MEALS	SUGAR ◯YES ◯NO
					COFFEE ◯YES ◯NO
					WATER ◯YES ◯NO
					WORKOUT ◯YES ◯NO

SUN	FATS	PROTEIN	CARBS	NUMBER OF MEALS	SUGAR ◯YES ◯NO
					COFFEE ◯YES ◯NO
					WATER ◯YES ◯NO
					WORKOUT ◯YES ◯NO

ENERGY LEVEL

	SUN	MON	TUE	WED	THU	FRI	SAT

OBSERVATIONS - HOW I FEEL

MY GOAL THIS WEEK

MEASUREMENT: WEIGHT:

CHEST................................WAIST................................HIPS................

DATA:		KETO DIET				

MON	FATS	PROTEIN	CARBS	NUMBER OF MEALS	SUGAR ◯ YES ◯ NO
					COFFEE ◯ YES ◯ NO
					WATER ◯ YES ◯ NO
					WORKOUT ◯ YES ◯ NO

TUE	FATS	PROTEIN	CARBS	NUMBER OF MEALS	SUGAR ◯ YES ◯ NO
					COFFEE ◯ YES ◯ NO
					WATER ◯ YES ◯ NO
					WORKOUT ◯ YES ◯ NO

WED	FATS	PROTEIN	CARBS	NUMBER OF MEALS	SUGAR ◯ YES ◯ NO
					COFFEE ◯ YES ◯ NO
					WATER ◯ YES ◯ NO
					WORKOUT ◯ YES ◯ NO

THU	FATS	PROTEIN	CARBS	NUMBER OF MEALS	SUGAR ◯ YES ◯ NO
					COFFEE ◯ YES ◯ NO
					WATER ◯ YES ◯ NO
					WORKOUT ◯ YES ◯ NO

FRI	FATS	PROTEIN	CARBS	NUMBER OF MEALS	SUGAR ◯ YES ◯ NO
					COFFEE ◯ YES ◯ NO
					WATER ◯ YES ◯ NO
					WORKOUT ◯ YES ◯ NO

NOTES & ACCOMPLISHMENT

DATA: _____	KETO DIET

SAT

	FATS	PROTEIN	CARBS	NUMBER OF MEALS		
SAT					SUGAR	◯ YES ◯ NO
					COFFEE	◯ YES ◯ NO
					WATER	◯ YES ◯ NO
					WORKOUT	◯ YES ◯ NO

	FATS	PROTEIN	CARBS	NUMBER OF MEALS		
SUN					SUGAR	◯ YES ◯ NO
					COFFEE	◯ YES ◯ NO
					WATER	◯ YES ◯ NO
					WORKOUT	◯ YES ◯ NO

ENERGY LEVEL

SUN	MON	TUE	WED	THU	FRI	SAT

OBSERVATIONS - HOW I FEEL

MY GOAL THIS WEEK

MEASUREMENT:	WEIGHT:
CHEST................WAIST................HIPS................	....

DATA:		KETO DIET				

	FATS	PROTEIN	CARBS	NUMBER OF MEALS		
MON					SUGAR ◯ YES ◯ NO	
					COFFEE ◯ YES ◯ NO	
					WATER ◯ YES ◯ NO	
					WORKOUT ◯ YES ◯ NO	
TUE	FATS	PROTEIN	CARBS	NUMBER OF MEALS	SUGAR ◯ YES ◯ NO	
					COFFEE ◯ YES ◯ NO	
					WATER ◯ YES ◯ NO	
					WORKOUT ◯ YES ◯ NO	
WED	FATS	PROTEIN	CARBS	NUMBER OF MEALS	SUGAR ◯ YES ◯ NO	
					COFFEE ◯ YES ◯ NO	
					WATER ◯ YES ◯ NO	
					WORKOUT ◯ YES ◯ NO	
THU	FATS	PROTEIN	CARBS	NUMBER OF MEALS	SUGAR ◯ YES ◯ NO	
					COFFEE ◯ YES ◯ NO	
					WATER ◯ YES ◯ NO	
					WORKOUT ◯ YES ◯ NO	
FRI	FATS	PROTEIN	CARBS	NUMBER OF MEALS	SUGAR ◯ YES ◯ NO	
					COFFEE ◯ YES ◯ NO	
					WATER ◯ YES ◯ NO	
					WORKOUT ◯ YES ◯ NO	

NOTES & ACCOMPLISHMENT

DATA:		KETO DIET					

SAT	FATS	PROTEIN	CARBS	NUMBER OF MEALS	SUGAR ⭕ YES ⭕ NO
					COFFEE ⭕ YES ⭕ NO
					WATER ⭕ YES ⭕ NO
					WORKOUT ⭕ YES ⭕ NO

SUN	FATS	PROTEIN	CARBS	NUMBER OF MEALS	SUGAR ⭕ YES ⭕ NO
					COFFEE ⭕ YES ⭕ NO
					WATER ⭕ YES ⭕ NO
					WORKOUT ⭕ YES ⭕ NO

ENERGY LEVEL

😄 🙂 😏 😮 😬 😵

SUN	MON	TUE	WED	THU	FRI	SAT

OBSERVATIONS - HOW I FEEL

MY GOAL THIS WEEK

MEASUREMENT:

CHEST................................WAIST................................HIPS................................

WEIGHT:

DATA:			KETO DIET		

MON	FATS	PROTEIN	CARBS	NUMBER OF MEALS	SUGAR ◯ YES ◯ NO
					COFFEE ◯ YES ◯ NO
					WATER ◯ YES ◯ NO
					WORKOUT ◯ YES ◯ NO

TUE	FATS	PROTEIN	CARBS	NUMBER OF MEALS	SUGAR ◯ YES ◯ NO
					COFFEE ◯ YES ◯ NO
					WATER ◯ YES ◯ NO
					WORKOUT ◯ YES ◯ NO

WED	FATS	PROTEIN	CARBS	NUMBER OF MEALS	SUGAR ◯ YES ◯ NO
					COFFEE ◯ YES ◯ NO
					WATER ◯ YES ◯ NO
					WORKOUT ◯ YES ◯ NO

THU	FATS	PROTEIN	CARBS	NUMBER OF MEALS	SUGAR ◯ YES ◯ NO
					COFFEE ◯ YES ◯ NO
					WATER ◯ YES ◯ NO
					WORKOUT ◯ YES ◯ NO

FRI	FATS	PROTEIN	CARBS	NUMBER OF MEALS	SUGAR ◯ YES ◯ NO
					COFFEE ◯ YES ◯ NO
					WATER ◯ YES ◯ NO
					WORKOUT ◯ YES ◯ NO

NOTES & ACCOMPLISHMENT

DATA:		KETO DIET					

	FATS	PROTEIN	CARBS	NUMBER OF MEALS	SUGAR ◯ YES ◯ NO
SAT					COFFEE ◯ YES ◯ NO
					WATER ◯ YES ◯ NO
					WORKOUT ◯ YES ◯ NO

	FATS	PROTEIN	CARBS	NUMBER OF MEALS	SUGAR ◯ YES ◯ NO
SUN					COFFEE ◯ YES ◯ NO
					WATER ◯ YES ◯ NO
					WORKOUT ◯ YES ◯ NO

ENERGY LEVEL

	SUN	MON	TUE	WED	THU	FRI	SAT

OBSERVATIONS - HOW I FEEL

MY GOAL THIS WEEK

MEASUREMENT:

WEIGHT:

CHEST.................... WAIST.................... HIPS....................

DATA:		KETO DIET				

MON

FATS	PROTEIN	CARBS	NUMBER OF MEALS	
				SUGAR ◯ YES ◯ NO
				COFFEE ◯ YES ◯ NO
				WATER ◯ YES ◯ NO
				WORKOUT ◯ YES ◯ NO

TUE

FATS	PROTEIN	CARBS	NUMBER OF MEALS	
				SUGAR ◯ YES ◯ NO
				COFFEE ◯ YES ◯ NO
				WATER ◯ YES ◯ NO
				WORKOUT ◯ YES ◯ NO

WED

FATS	PROTEIN	CARBS	NUMBER OF MEALS	
				SUGAR ◯ YES ◯ NO
				COFFEE ◯ YES ◯ NO
				WATER ◯ YES ◯ NO
				WORKOUT ◯ YES ◯ NO

THU

FATS	PROTEIN	CARBS	NUMBER OF MEALS	
				SUGAR ◯ YES ◯ NO
				COFFEE ◯ YES ◯ NO
				WATER ◯ YES ◯ NO
				WORKOUT ◯ YES ◯ NO

FRI

FATS	PROTEIN	CARBS	NUMBER OF MEALS	
				SUGAR ◯ YES ◯ NO
				COFFEE ◯ YES ◯ NO
				WATER ◯ YES ◯ NO
				WORKOUT ◯ YES ◯ NO

NOTES & ACCOMPLISHMENT

DATA: _____	**KETO DIET**			

SAT

FATS	PROTEIN	CARBS	NUMBER OF MEALS	
				SUGAR ○ YES ○ NO
				COFFEE ○ YES ○ NO
				WATER ○ YES ○ NO
				WORKOUT ○ YES ○ NO

SUN

FATS	PROTEIN	CARBS	NUMBER OF MEALS	
				SUGAR ○ YES ○ NO
				COFFEE ○ YES ○ NO
				WATER ○ YES ○ NO
				WORKOUT ○ YES ○ NO

ENERGY LEVEL

😊 🙂 😏 😯 😬 😵

SUN	MON	TUE	WED	THU	FRI	SAT

OBSERVATIONS - HOW I FEEL

MY GOAL THIS WEEK

MEASUREMENT:

CHEST................................WAIST................................HIPS................................

WEIGHT:

DATA:		KETO DIET				

MON

FATS	PROTEIN	CARBS	NUMBER OF MEALS	SUGAR ○ YES ○ NO
				COFFEE ○ YES ○ NO
				WATER ○ YES ○ NO
				WORKOUT ○ YES ○ NO

TUE

FATS	PROTEIN	CARBS	NUMBER OF MEALS	SUGAR ○ YES ○ NO
				COFFEE ○ YES ○ NO
				WATER ○ YES ○ NO
				WORKOUT ○ YES ○ NO

WED

FATS	PROTEIN	CARBS	NUMBER OF MEALS	SUGAR ○ YES ○ NO
				COFFEE ○ YES ○ NO
				WATER ○ YES ○ NO
				WORKOUT ○ YES ○ NO

THU

FATS	PROTEIN	CARBS	NUMBER OF MEALS	SUGAR ○ YES ○ NO
				COFFEE ○ YES ○ NO
				WATER ○ YES ○ NO
				WORKOUT ○ YES ○ NO

FRI

FATS	PROTEIN	CARBS	NUMBER OF MEALS	SUGAR ○ YES ○ NO
				COFFEE ○ YES ○ NO
				WATER ○ YES ○ NO
				WORKOUT ○ YES ○ NO

NOTES & ACCOMPLISHMENT

KETO DIET

SAT	FATS	PROTEIN	CARBS	NUMBER OF MEALS	SUGAR ⭘ YES ⭘ NO
					COFFEE ⭘ YES ⭘ NO
					WATER ⭘ YES ⭘ NO
					WORKOUT ⭘ YES ⭘ NO

SUN	FATS	PROTEIN	CARBS	NUMBER OF MEALS	SUGAR ⭘ YES ⭘ NO
					COFFEE ⭘ YES ⭘ NO
					WATER ⭘ YES ⭘ NO
					WORKOUT ⭘ YES ⭘ NO

ENERGY LEVEL

SUN	MON	TUE	WED	THU	FRI	SAT

OBSERVATIONS - HOW I FEEL

MY GOAL THIS WEEK

MEASUREMENT:

WEIGHT:

CHEST.................... WAIST.................... HIPS....................

DATA:		KETO DIET				

MON	FATS	PROTEIN	CARBS	NUMBER OF MEALS	SUGAR ◯ YES ◯ NO
					COFFEE ◯ YES ◯ NO
					WATER ◯ YES ◯ NO
					WORKOUT ◯ YES ◯ NO

TUE	FATS	PROTEIN	CARBS	NUMBER OF MEALS	SUGAR ◯ YES ◯ NO
					COFFEE ◯ YES ◯ NO
					WATER ◯ YES ◯ NO
					WORKOUT ◯ YES ◯ NO

WED	FATS	PROTEIN	CARBS	NUMBER OF MEALS	SUGAR ◯ YES ◯ NO
					COFFEE ◯ YES ◯ NO
					WATER ◯ YES ◯ NO
					WORKOUT ◯ YES ◯ NO

THU	FATS	PROTEIN	CARBS	NUMBER OF MEALS	SUGAR ◯ YES ◯ NO
					COFFEE ◯ YES ◯ NO
					WATER ◯ YES ◯ NO
					WORKOUT ◯ YES ◯ NO

FRI	FATS	PROTEIN	CARBS	NUMBER OF MEALS	SUGAR ◯ YES ◯ NO
					COFFEE ◯ YES ◯ NO
					WATER ◯ YES ◯ NO
					WORKOUT ◯ YES ◯ NO

NOTES & ACCOMPLISHMENT

SAT	FATS	PROTEIN	CARBS	NUMBER OF MEALS	SUGAR	○ YES ○ NO
					COFFEE	○ YES ○ NO
					WATER	○ YES ○ NO
					WORKOUT	○ YES ○ NO

SUN	FATS	PROTEIN	CARBS	NUMBER OF MEALS	SUGAR	○ YES ○ NO
					COFFEE	○ YES ○ NO
					WATER	○ YES ○ NO
					WORKOUT	○ YES ○ NO

ENERGY LEVEL

	SUN	MON	TUE	WED	THU	FRI	SAT

OBSERVATIONS - HOW I FEEL

MY GOAL THIS WEEK

MEASUREMENT:

CHEST................................WAIST................................HIPS................................

WEIGHT:

DATA:				KETO DIET				

	FATS	PROTEIN	CARBS	NUMBER OF MEALS		
MON					SUGAR ○ YES ○ NO	
					COFFEE ○ YES ○ NO	
					WATER ○ YES ○ NO	
					WORKOUT ○ YES ○ NO	
TUE	FATS	PROTEIN	CARBS	NUMBER OF MEALS	SUGAR ○ YES ○ NO	
					COFFEE ○ YES ○ NO	
					WATER ○ YES ○ NO	
					WORKOUT ○ YES ○ NO	
WED	FATS	PROTEIN	CARBS	NUMBER OF MEALS	SUGAR ○ YES ○ NO	
					COFFEE ○ YES ○ NO	
					WATER ○ YES ○ NO	
					WORKOUT ○ YES ○ NO	
THU	FATS	PROTEIN	CARBS	NUMBER OF MEALS	SUGAR ○ YES ○ NO	
					COFFEE ○ YES ○ NO	
					WATER ○ YES ○ NO	
					WORKOUT ○ YES ○ NO	
FRI	FATS	PROTEIN	CARBS	NUMBER OF MEALS	SUGAR ○ YES ○ NO	
					COFFEE ○ YES ○ NO	
					WATER ○ YES ○ NO	
					WORKOUT ○ YES ○ NO	

NOTES & ACCOMPLISHMENT

SAT	FATS	PROTEIN	CARBS	NUMBER OF MEALS	SUGAR ⭘ YES ⭘ NO
					COFFEE ⭘ YES ⭘ NO
					WATER ⭘ YES ⭘ NO
					WORKOUT ⭘ YES ⭘ NO

SUN	FATS	PROTEIN	CARBS	NUMBER OF MEALS	SUGAR ⭘ YES ⭘ NO
					COFFEE ⭘ YES ⭘ NO
					WATER ⭘ YES ⭘ NO
					WORKOUT ⭘ YES ⭘ NO

ENERGY LEVEL

SUN	MON	TUE	WED	THU	FRI	SAT

OBSERVATIONS - HOW I FEEL

MY GOAL THIS WEEK

MEASUREMENT:

CHEST............................WAIST...............................HIPS............................

WEIGHT:

DATA:		KETO DIET				

	FATS	PROTEIN	CARBS	NUMBER OF MEALS		
MON					SUGAR ◯ YES ◯ NO	
					COFFEE ◯ YES ◯ NO	
					WATER ◯ YES ◯ NO	
					WORKOUT ◯ YES ◯ NO	
	FATS	PROTEIN	CARBS	NUMBER OF MEALS		
TUE					SUGAR ◯ YES ◯ NO	
					COFFEE ◯ YES ◯ NO	
					WATER ◯ YES ◯ NO	
					WORKOUT ◯ YES ◯ NO	
	FATS	PROTEIN	CARBS	NUMBER OF MEALS		
WED					SUGAR ◯ YES ◯ NO	
					COFFEE ◯ YES ◯ NO	
					WATER ◯ YES ◯ NO	
					WORKOUT ◯ YES ◯ NO	
	FATS	PROTEIN	CARBS	NUMBER OF MEALS		
THU					SUGAR ◯ YES ◯ NO	
					COFFEE ◯ YES ◯ NO	
					WATER ◯ YES ◯ NO	
					WORKOUT ◯ YES ◯ NO	
	FATS	PROTEIN	CARBS	NUMBER OF MEALS		
FRI					SUGAR ◯ YES ◯ NO	
					COFFEE ◯ YES ◯ NO	
					WATER ◯ YES ◯ NO	
					WORKOUT ◯ YES ◯ NO	

NOTES & ACCOMPLISHMENT

DATA: _____	KETO DIET

SAT

	FATS	PROTEIN	CARBS	NUMBER OF MEALS

SUGAR	○ YES ○ NO
COFFEE	○ YES ○ NO
WATER	○ YES ○ NO
WORKOUT	○ YES ○ NO

SUN

	FATS	PROTEIN	CARBS	NUMBER OF MEALS

SUGAR	○ YES ○ NO
COFFEE	○ YES ○ NO
WATER	○ YES ○ NO
WORKOUT	○ YES ○ NO

ENERGY LEVEL

SUN	MON	TUE	WED	THU	FRI	SAT

OBSERVATIONS - HOW I FEEL

MY GOAL THIS WEEK

MEASUREMENT:	WEIGHT:
CHEST................ WAIST................ HIPS................	....

DATA:		KETO DIET				

MON	FATS	PROTEIN	CARBS	NUMBER OF MEALS	SUGAR ○ YES ○ NO
					COFFEE ○ YES ○ NO
					WATER ○ YES ○ NO
					WORKOUT ○ YES ○ NO

TUE	FATS	PROTEIN	CARBS	NUMBER OF MEALS	SUGAR ○ YES ○ NO
					COFFEE ○ YES ○ NO
					WATER ○ YES ○ NO
					WORKOUT ○ YES ○ NO

WED	FATS	PROTEIN	CARBS	NUMBER OF MEALS	SUGAR ○ YES ○ NO
					COFFEE ○ YES ○ NO
					WATER ○ YES ○ NO
					WORKOUT ○ YES ○ NO

THU	FATS	PROTEIN	CARBS	NUMBER OF MEALS	SUGAR ○ YES ○ NO
					COFFEE ○ YES ○ NO
					WATER ○ YES ○ NO
					WORKOUT ○ YES ○ NO

FRI	FATS	PROTEIN	CARBS	NUMBER OF MEALS	SUGAR ○ YES ○ NO
					COFFEE ○ YES ○ NO
					WATER ○ YES ○ NO
					WORKOUT ○ YES ○ NO

NOTES & ACCOMPLISHMENT

DATA:		KETO DIET				

SAT	FATS	PROTEIN	CARBS	NUMBER OF MEALS	SUGAR ⭕ YES ⭕ NO
					COFFEE ⭕ YES ⭕ NO
					WATER ⭕ YES ⭕ NO
					WORKOUT ⭕ YES ⭕ NO

SUN	FATS	PROTEIN	CARBS	NUMBER OF MEALS	SUGAR ⭕ YES ⭕ NO
					COFFEE ⭕ YES ⭕ NO
					WATER ⭕ YES ⭕ NO
					WORKOUT ⭕ YES ⭕ NO

ENERGY LEVEL

SUN	MON	TUE	WED	THU	FRI	SAT

OBSERVATIONS - HOW I FEEL

MY GOAL THIS WEEK

MEASUREMENT:	WEIGHT:
CHEST................WAIST................HIPS................	

DATA:		KETO DIET				

MON

FATS	PROTEIN	CARBS	NUMBER OF MEALS		
				SUGAR ○YES ○NO
				COFFEE ○YES ○NO
				WATER ○YES ○NO
				WORKOUT ○YES ○NO

TUE

FATS	PROTEIN	CARBS	NUMBER OF MEALS		
				SUGAR ○YES ○NO
				COFFEE ○YES ○NO
				WATER ○YES ○NO
				WORKOUT ○YES ○NO

WED

FATS	PROTEIN	CARBS	NUMBER OF MEALS		
				SUGAR ○YES ○NO
				COFFEE ○YES ○NO
				WATER ○YES ○NO
				WORKOUT ○YES ○NO

THU

FATS	PROTEIN	CARBS	NUMBER OF MEALS		
				SUGAR ○YES ○NO
				COFFEE ○YES ○NO
				WATER ○YES ○NO
				WORKOUT ○YES ○NO

FRI

FATS	PROTEIN	CARBS	NUMBER OF MEALS		
				SUGAR ○YES ○NO
				COFFEE ○YES ○NO
				WATER ○YES ○NO
				WORKOUT ○YES ○NO

NOTES & ACCOMPLISHMENT

SAT	FATS	PROTEIN	CARBS	NUMBER OF MEALS	SUGAR ◯ YES ◯ NO
					COFFEE ◯ YES ◯ NO
					WATER ◯ YES ◯ NO
					WORKOUT ◯ YES ◯ NO

SUN	FATS	PROTEIN	CARBS	NUMBER OF MEALS	SUGAR ◯ YES ◯ NO
					COFFEE ◯ YES ◯ NO
					WATER ◯ YES ◯ NO
					WORKOUT ◯ YES ◯ NO

ENERGY LEVEL

SUN	MON	TUE	WED	THU	FRI	SAT

OBSERVATIONS - HOW I FEEL

MY GOAL THIS WEEK

MEASUREMENT:

CHEST................................WAIST................................HIPS................................

WEIGHT:

DATA:	KETO DIET				

	FATS	PROTEIN	CARBS	NUMBER OF MEALS	
MON					SUGAR ◯ YES ◯ NO
					COFFEE ◯ YES ◯ NO
					WATER ◯ YES ◯ NO
					WORKOUT ◯ YES ◯ NO

	FATS	PROTEIN	CARBS	NUMBER OF MEALS	
TUE					SUGAR ◯ YES ◯ NO
					COFFEE ◯ YES ◯ NO
					WATER ◯ YES ◯ NO
					WORKOUT ◯ YES ◯ NO

	FATS	PROTEIN	CARBS	NUMBER OF MEALS	
WED					SUGAR ◯ YES ◯ NO
					COFFEE ◯ YES ◯ NO
					WATER ◯ YES ◯ NO
					WORKOUT ◯ YES ◯ NO

	FATS	PROTEIN	CARBS	NUMBER OF MEALS	
THU					SUGAR ◯ YES ◯ NO
					COFFEE ◯ YES ◯ NO
					WATER ◯ YES ◯ NO
					WORKOUT ◯ YES ◯ NO

	FATS	PROTEIN	CARBS	NUMBER OF MEALS	
FRI					SUGAR ◯ YES ◯ NO
					COFFEE ◯ YES ◯ NO
					WATER ◯ YES ◯ NO
					WORKOUT ◯ YES ◯ NO

NOTES & ACCOMPLISHMENT

| DATA: | | **KETO DIET** | | | | |

SAT	FATS	PROTEIN	CARBS	NUMBER OF MEALS	
					SUGAR ◯ YES ◯ NO
					COFFEE ◯ YES ◯ NO
					WATER ◯ YES ◯ NO
					WORKOUT ◯ YES ◯ NO

SUN	FATS	PROTEIN	CARBS	NUMBER OF MEALS	
					SUGAR ◯ YES ◯ NO
					COFFEE ◯ YES ◯ NO
					WATER ◯ YES ◯ NO
					WORKOUT ◯ YES ◯ NO

ENERGY LEVEL

SUN	MON	TUE	WED	THU	FRI	SAT

OBSERVATIONS - HOW I FEEL

MY GOAL THIS WEEK

MEASUREMENT:

WEIGHT:

CHEST.............................WAIST...............................HIPS...........................

DATA:		KETO DIET				

MON

FATS	PROTEIN	CARBS	NUMBER OF MEALS	SUGAR ◯ YES ◯ NO
				COFFEE ◯ YES ◯ NO
				WATER ◯ YES ◯ NO
				WORKOUT ◯ YES ◯ NO

TUE

FATS	PROTEIN	CARBS	NUMBER OF MEALS	SUGAR ◯ YES ◯ NO
				COFFEE ◯ YES ◯ NO
				WATER ◯ YES ◯ NO
				WORKOUT ◯ YES ◯ NO

WED

FATS	PROTEIN	CARBS	NUMBER OF MEALS	SUGAR ◯ YES ◯ NO
				COFFEE ◯ YES ◯ NO
				WATER ◯ YES ◯ NO
				WORKOUT ◯ YES ◯ NO

THU

FATS	PROTEIN	CARBS	NUMBER OF MEALS	SUGAR ◯ YES ◯ NO
				COFFEE ◯ YES ◯ NO
				WATER ◯ YES ◯ NO
				WORKOUT ◯ YES ◯ NO

FRI

FATS	PROTEIN	CARBS	NUMBER OF MEALS	SUGAR ◯ YES ◯ NO
				COFFEE ◯ YES ◯ NO
				WATER ◯ YES ◯ NO
				WORKOUT ◯ YES ◯ NO

NOTES & ACCOMPLISHMENT

SAT	FATS	PROTEIN	CARBS	NUMBER OF MEALS	SUGAR ◯ YES ◯ NO
					COFFEE ◯ YES ◯ NO
					WATER ◯ YES ◯ NO
					WORKOUT ◯ YES ◯ NO

SUN	FATS	PROTEIN	CARBS	NUMBER OF MEALS	SUGAR ◯ YES ◯ NO
					COFFEE ◯ YES ◯ NO
					WATER ◯ YES ◯ NO
					WORKOUT ◯ YES ◯ NO

ENERGY LEVEL

SUN	MON	TUE	WED	THU	FRI	SAT

OBSERVATIONS - HOW I FEEL

MY GOAL THIS WEEK

MEASUREMENT:

CHEST................................WAIST................................HIPS................................

WEIGHT:

DATA:		KETO DIET				

	FATS	PROTEIN	CARBS	NUMBER OF MEALS		
MON					SUGAR ◯YES ◯NO	
					COFFEE ◯YES ◯NO	
					WATER ◯YES ◯NO	
					WORKOUT ◯YES ◯NO	
	FATS	PROTEIN	CARBS	NUMBER OF MEALS		
TUE					SUGAR ◯YES ◯NO	
					COFFEE ◯YES ◯NO	
					WATER ◯YES ◯NO	
					WORKOUT ◯YES ◯NO	
	FATS	PROTEIN	CARBS	NUMBER OF MEALS		
WED					SUGAR ◯YES ◯NO	
					COFFEE ◯YES ◯NO	
					WATER ◯YES ◯NO	
					WORKOUT ◯YES ◯NO	
	FATS	PROTEIN	CARBS	NUMBER OF MEALS		
THU					SUGAR ◯YES ◯NO	
					COFFEE ◯YES ◯NO	
					WATER ◯YES ◯NO	
					WORKOUT ◯YES ◯NO	
	FATS	PROTEIN	CARBS	NUMBER OF MEALS		
FRI					SUGAR ◯YES ◯NO	
					COFFEE ◯YES ◯NO	
					WATER ◯YES ◯NO	
					WORKOUT ◯YES ◯NO	

NOTES & ACCOMPLISHMENT

DATA:		**KETO DIET**			

	FATS	PROTEIN	CARBS	NUMBER OF MEALS	
SAT					SUGAR ○ YES ○ NO
					COFFEE ○ YES ○ NO
					WATER ○ YES ○ NO
					WORKOUT ○ YES ○ NO

	FATS	PROTEIN	CARBS	NUMBER OF MEALS	
SUN					SUGAR ○ YES ○ NO
					COFFEE ○ YES ○ NO
					WATER ○ YES ○ NO
					WORKOUT ○ YES ○ NO

ENERGY LEVEL

SUN	MON	TUE	WED	THU	FRI	SAT

OBSERVATIONS - HOW I FEEL

MY GOAL THIS WEEK

MEASUREMENT:

WEIGHT:

CHEST................................WAIST..HIPS..................

DATA:		KETO DIET				

MON

FATS	PROTEIN	CARBS	NUMBER OF MEALS		
				SUGAR ○YES ○NO
				COFFEE ○YES ○NO
				WATER ○YES ○NO
				WORKOUT ○YES ○NO

TUE

FATS	PROTEIN	CARBS	NUMBER OF MEALS		
				SUGAR ○YES ○NO
				COFFEE ○YES ○NO
				WATER ○YES ○NO
				WORKOUT ○YES ○NO

WED

FATS	PROTEIN	CARBS	NUMBER OF MEALS		
				SUGAR ○YES ○NO
				COFFEE ○YES ○NO
				WATER ○YES ○NO
				WORKOUT ○YES ○NO

THU

FATS	PROTEIN	CARBS	NUMBER OF MEALS		
				SUGAR ○YES ○NO
				COFFEE ○YES ○NO
				WATER ○YES ○NO
				WORKOUT ○YES ○NO

FRI

FATS	PROTEIN	CARBS	NUMBER OF MEALS		
				SUGAR ○YES ○NO
				COFFEE ○YES ○NO
				WATER ○YES ○NO
				WORKOUT ○YES ○NO

NOTES & ACCOMPLISHMENT

DATA:		KETO DIET				

SAT	FATS	PROTEIN	CARBS	NUMBER OF MEALS	SUGAR ○YES ○NO
					COFFEE ○YES ○NO
					WATER ○YES ○NO
					WORKOUT○YES ○NO

SUN	FATS	PROTEIN	CARBS	NUMBER OF MEALS	SUGAR ○YES ○NO
					COFFEE ○YES ○NO
					WATER ○YES ○NO
					WORKOUT○YES ○NO

ENERGY LEVEL

	SUN	MON	TUE	WED	THU	FRI	SAT

OBSERVATIONS - HOW I FEEL

MY GOAL THIS WEEK

MEASUREMENT:	WEIGHT:
CHEST...................WAIST...................HIPS..................	

DATA:		KETO DIET				
MON	FATS	PROTEIN	CARBS	NUMBER OF MEALS	SUGAR ○ YES ○ NO
					COFFEE ○ YES ○ NO
					WATER ○ YES ○ NO
					WORKOUT ○ YES ○ NO
TUE	FATS	PROTEIN	CARBS	NUMBER OF MEALS	SUGAR ○ YES ○ NO
					COFFEE ○ YES ○ NO
					WATER ○ YES ○ NO
					WORKOUT ○ YES ○ NO
WED	FATS	PROTEIN	CARBS	NUMBER OF MEALS	SUGAR ○ YES ○ NO
					COFFEE ○ YES ○ NO
					WATER ○ YES ○ NO
					WORKOUT ○ YES ○ NO
THU	FATS	PROTEIN	CARBS	NUMBER OF MEALS	SUGAR ○ YES ○ NO
					COFFEE ○ YES ○ NO
					WATER ○ YES ○ NO
					WORKOUT ○ YES ○ NO
FRI	FATS	PROTEIN	CARBS	NUMBER OF MEALS	SUGAR ○ YES ○ NO
					COFFEE ○ YES ○ NO
					WATER ○ YES ○ NO
					WORKOUT ○ YES ○ NO

NOTES & ACCOMPLISHMENT

DATA:		KETO DIET				

SAT	FATS	PROTEIN	CARBS	NUMBER OF MEALS	SUGAR ◯ YES ◯ NO
					COFFEE ◯ YES ◯ NO
					WATER ◯ YES ◯ NO
					WORKOUT ◯ YES ◯ NO

SUN	FATS	PROTEIN	CARBS	NUMBER OF MEALS	SUGAR ◯ YES ◯ NO
					COFFEE ◯ YES ◯ NO
					WATER ◯ YES ◯ NO
					WORKOUT ◯ YES ◯ NO

ENERGY LEVEL

	SUN	MON	TUE	WED	THU	FRI	SAT

OBSERVATIONS - HOW I FEEL

MY GOAL THIS WEEK

MEASUREMENT:

CHEST.................................WAIST.................................HIPS.................................

WEIGHT:

DATA:		KETO DIET				

MON	FATS	PROTEIN	CARBS	NUMBER OF MEALS	SUGAR ◯ YES ◯ NO
					COFFEE ◯ YES ◯ NO
					WATER ◯ YES ◯ NO
					WORKOUT ◯ YES ◯ NO

TUE	FATS	PROTEIN	CARBS	NUMBER OF MEALS	SUGAR ◯ YES ◯ NO
					COFFEE ◯ YES ◯ NO
					WATER ◯ YES ◯ NO
					WORKOUT ◯ YES ◯ NO

WED	FATS	PROTEIN	CARBS	NUMBER OF MEALS	SUGAR ◯ YES ◯ NO
					COFFEE ◯ YES ◯ NO
					WATER ◯ YES ◯ NO
					WORKOUT ◯ YES ◯ NO

THU	FATS	PROTEIN	CARBS	NUMBER OF MEALS	SUGAR ◯ YES ◯ NO
					COFFEE ◯ YES ◯ NO
					WATER ◯ YES ◯ NO
					WORKOUT ◯ YES ◯ NO

FRI	FATS	PROTEIN	CARBS	NUMBER OF MEALS	SUGAR ◯ YES ◯ NO
					COFFEE ◯ YES ◯ NO
					WATER ◯ YES ◯ NO
					WORKOUT ◯ YES ◯ NO

NOTES & ACCOMPLISHMENT

DATA:			KETO DIET		

SAT

FATS	PROTEIN	CARBS	NUMBER OF MEALS

SUGAR	◯ YES ◯ NO
COFFEE	◯ YES ◯ NO
WATER	◯ YES ◯ NO
WORKOUT	◯ YES ◯ NO

SUN

FATS	PROTEIN	CARBS	NUMBER OF MEALS

SUGAR	◯ YES ◯ NO
COFFEE	◯ YES ◯ NO
WATER	◯ YES ◯ NO
WORKOUT	◯ YES ◯ NO

ENERGY LEVEL

SUN	MON	TUE	WED	THU	FRI	SAT

OBSERVATIONS - HOW I FEEL

MY GOAL THIS WEEK

MEASUREMENT:	WEIGHT:
CHEST............................WAIST............................HIPS............................	....

DATA:		KETO DIET			

MON

FATS	PROTEIN	CARBS	NUMBER OF MEALS	
				SUGAR ○ YES ○ NO
				COFFEE ○ YES ○ NO
				WATER ○ YES ○ NO
				WORKOUT ○ YES ○ NO

TUE

FATS	PROTEIN	CARBS	NUMBER OF MEALS	
				SUGAR ○ YES ○ NO
				COFFEE ○ YES ○ NO
				WATER ○ YES ○ NO
				WORKOUT ○ YES ○ NO

WED

FATS	PROTEIN	CARBS	NUMBER OF MEALS	
				SUGAR ○ YES ○ NO
				COFFEE ○ YES ○ NO
				WATER ○ YES ○ NO
				WORKOUT ○ YES ○ NO

THU

FATS	PROTEIN	CARBS	NUMBER OF MEALS	
				SUGAR ○ YES ○ NO
				COFFEE ○ YES ○ NO
				WATER ○ YES ○ NO
				WORKOUT ○ YES ○ NO

FRI

FATS	PROTEIN	CARBS	NUMBER OF MEALS	
				SUGAR ○ YES ○ NO
				COFFEE ○ YES ○ NO
				WATER ○ YES ○ NO
				WORKOUT ○ YES ○ NO

NOTES & ACCOMPLISHMENT

DATA:		KETO DIET				

SAT

FATS	PROTEIN	CARBS	NUMBER OF MEALS

SUGAR	◯ YES ◯ NO
COFFEE	◯ YES ◯ NO
WATER	◯ YES ◯ NO
WORKOUT	◯ YES ◯ NO

SUN

FATS	PROTEIN	CARBS	NUMBER OF MEALS

SUGAR	◯ YES ◯ NO
COFFEE	◯ YES ◯ NO
WATER	◯ YES ◯ NO
WORKOUT	◯ YES ◯ NO

ENERGY LEVEL

SUN	MON	TUE	WED	THU	FRI	SAT

OBSERVATIONS - HOW I FEEL

MY GOAL THIS WEEK

MEASUREMENT:

CHEST................................WAIST................................HIPS................................

WEIGHT:

DATA:		KETO DIET				

	FATS	PROTEIN	CARBS	NUMBER OF MEALS		
MON					SUGAR ○ YES ○ NO	
					COFFEE ○ YES ○ NO	
					WATER ○ YES ○ NO	
					WORKOUT ○ YES ○ NO	

	FATS	PROTEIN	CARBS	NUMBER OF MEALS		
TUE					SUGAR ○ YES ○ NO	
					COFFEE ○ YES ○ NO	
					WATER ○ YES ○ NO	
					WORKOUT ○ YES ○ NO	

	FATS	PROTEIN	CARBS	NUMBER OF MEALS		
WED					SUGAR ○ YES ○ NO	
					COFFEE ○ YES ○ NO	
					WATER ○ YES ○ NO	
					WORKOUT ○ YES ○ NO	

	FATS	PROTEIN	CARBS	NUMBER OF MEALS		
THU					SUGAR ○ YES ○ NO	
					COFFEE ○ YES ○ NO	
					WATER ○ YES ○ NO	
					WORKOUT ○ YES ○ NO	

	FATS	PROTEIN	CARBS	NUMBER OF MEALS		
FRI					SUGAR ○ YES ○ NO	
					COFFEE ○ YES ○ NO	
					WATER ○ YES ○ NO	
					WORKOUT ○ YES ○ NO	

NOTES & ACCOMPLISHMENT

KETO DIET

SAT	FATS	PROTEIN	CARBS	NUMBER OF MEALS	SUGAR ○ YES ○ NO
					COFFEE ○ YES ○ NO
					WATER ○ YES ○ NO
					WORKOUT ○ YES ○ NO

SUN	FATS	PROTEIN	CARBS	NUMBER OF MEALS	SUGAR ○ YES ○ NO
					COFFEE ○ YES ○ NO
					WATER ○ YES ○ NO
					WORKOUT ○ YES ○ NO

ENERGY LEVEL

SUN	MON	TUE	WED	THU	FRI	SAT

OBSERVATIONS - HOW I FEEL

MY GOAL THIS WEEK

MEASUREMENT:

WEIGHT:

CHEST.................... WAIST.................... HIPS....................

| DATA: | | KETO DIET | | | |

	FATS	PROTEIN	CARBS	NUMBER OF MEALS	
MON					SUGAR ◯ YES ◯ NO
					COFFEE ◯ YES ◯ NO
					WATER ◯ YES ◯ NO
					WORKOUT ◯ YES ◯ NO

	FATS	PROTEIN	CARBS	NUMBER OF MEALS	
TUE					SUGAR ◯ YES ◯ NO
					COFFEE ◯ YES ◯ NO
					WATER ◯ YES ◯ NO
					WORKOUT ◯ YES ◯ NO

	FATS	PROTEIN	CARBS	NUMBER OF MEALS	
WED					SUGAR ◯ YES ◯ NO
					COFFEE ◯ YES ◯ NO
					WATER ◯ YES ◯ NO
					WORKOUT ◯ YES ◯ NO

	FATS	PROTEIN	CARBS	NUMBER OF MEALS	
THU					SUGAR ◯ YES ◯ NO
					COFFEE ◯ YES ◯ NO
					WATER ◯ YES ◯ NO
					WORKOUT ◯ YES ◯ NO

	FATS	PROTEIN	CARBS	NUMBER OF MEALS	
FRI					SUGAR ◯ YES ◯ NO
					COFFEE ◯ YES ◯ NO
					WATER ◯ YES ◯ NO
					WORKOUT ◯ YES ◯ NO

NOTES & ACCOMPLISHMENT

SAT	FATS	PROTEIN	CARBS	NUMBER OF MEALS	SUGAR ◯ YES ◯ NO
					COFFEE ◯ YES ◯ NO
					WATER ◯ YES ◯ NO
					WORKOUT ◯ YES ◯ NO

SUN	FATS	PROTEIN	CARBS	NUMBER OF MEALS	SUGAR ◯ YES ◯ NO
					COFFEE ◯ YES ◯ NO
					WATER ◯ YES ◯ NO
					WORKOUT ◯ YES ◯ NO

ENERGY LEVEL

SUN	MON	TUE	WED	THU	FRI	SAT

OBSERVATIONS - HOW I FEEL

MY GOAL THIS WEEK

MEASUREMENT:

WEIGHT:

CHEST................................WAIST................................HIPS................................

DATA:		**KETO DIET**					

	FATS	PROTEIN	CARBS	NUMBER OF MEALS			
MON					SUGAR ○ YES ○ NO		
					COFFEE ○ YES ○ NO		
					WATER ○ YES ○ NO		
					WORKOUT ○ YES ○ NO		

	FATS	PROTEIN	CARBS	NUMBER OF MEALS			
TUE					SUGAR ○ YES ○ NO		
					COFFEE ○ YES ○ NO		
					WATER ○ YES ○ NO		
					WORKOUT ○ YES ○ NO		

	FATS	PROTEIN	CARBS	NUMBER OF MEALS			
WED					SUGAR ○ YES ○ NO		
					COFFEE ○ YES ○ NO		
					WATER ○ YES ○ NO		
					WORKOUT ○ YES ○ NO		

	FATS	PROTEIN	CARBS	NUMBER OF MEALS			
THU					SUGAR ○ YES ○ NO		
					COFFEE ○ YES ○ NO		
					WATER ○ YES ○ NO		
					WORKOUT ○ YES ○ NO		

	FATS	PROTEIN	CARBS	NUMBER OF MEALS			
FRI					SUGAR ○ YES ○ NO		
					COFFEE ○ YES ○ NO		
					WATER ○ YES ○ NO		
					WORKOUT ○ YES ○ NO		

NOTES & ACCOMPLISHMENT

DATA:		KETO DIET				

SAT

FATS	PROTEIN	CARBS	NUMBER OF MEALS	
				SUGAR ○YES ○NO
				COFFEE ○YES ○NO
				WATER ○YES ○NO
				WORKOUT ○YES ○NO

SUN

FATS	PROTEIN	CARBS	NUMBER OF MEALS	
				SUGAR ○YES ○NO
				COFFEE ○YES ○NO
				WATER ○YES ○NO
				WORKOUT ○YES ○NO

ENERGY LEVEL

SUN	MON	TUE	WED	THU	FRI	SAT

OBSERVATIONS - HOW I FEEL

MY GOAL THIS WEEK

MEASUREMENT:	WEIGHT:
CHEST............................WAIST............................HIPS............................	....

DATA:		KETO DIET				

	FATS	PROTEIN	CARBS	NUMBER OF MEALS		
MON					SUGAR ◯YES ◯NO	
					COFFEE ◯YES ◯NO	
					WATER ◯YES ◯NO	
					WORKOUT ◯YES ◯NO	

	FATS	PROTEIN	CARBS	NUMBER OF MEALS		
TUE					SUGAR ◯YES ◯NO	
					COFFEE ◯YES ◯NO	
					WATER ◯YES ◯NO	
					WORKOUT ◯YES ◯NO	

	FATS	PROTEIN	CARBS	NUMBER OF MEALS		
WED					SUGAR ◯YES ◯NO	
					COFFEE ◯YES ◯NO	
					WATER ◯YES ◯NO	
					WORKOUT ◯YES ◯NO	

	FATS	PROTEIN	CARBS	NUMBER OF MEALS		
THU					SUGAR ◯YES ◯NO	
					COFFEE ◯YES ◯NO	
					WATER ◯YES ◯NO	
					WORKOUT ◯YES ◯NO	

	FATS	PROTEIN	CARBS	NUMBER OF MEALS		
FRI					SUGAR ◯YES ◯NO	
					COFFEE ◯YES ◯NO	
					WATER ◯YES ◯NO	
					WORKOUT ◯YES ◯NO	

NOTES & ACCOMPLISHMENT

DATA: _____   **KETO DIET**

SAT	FATS	PROTEIN	CARBS	NUMBER OF MEALS	SUGAR ○ YES ○ NO
					COFFEE ○ YES ○ NO
					WATER ○ YES ○ NO
					WORKOUT ○ YES ○ NO

SUN	FATS	PROTEIN	CARBS	NUMBER OF MEALS	SUGAR ○ YES ○ NO
					COFFEE ○ YES ○ NO
					WATER ○ YES ○ NO
					WORKOUT ○ YES ○ NO

ENERGY LEVEL

SUN	MON	TUE	WED	THU	FRI	SAT

OBSERVATIONS - HOW I FEEL

MY GOAL THIS WEEK

MEASUREMENT:

WEIGHT:

CHEST.................... WAIST.................... HIPS....................

DATA:		**KETO DIET**				

	FATS	PROTEIN	CARBS	NUMBER OF MEALS	
MON					SUGAR ◯YES ◯NO
					COFFEE ◯YES ◯NO
					WATER ◯YES ◯NO
					WORKOUT◯YES ◯NO

	FATS	PROTEIN	CARBS	NUMBER OF MEALS	
TUE					SUGAR ◯YES ◯NO
					COFFEE ◯YES ◯NO
					WATER ◯YES ◯NO
					WORKOUT◯YES ◯NO

	FATS	PROTEIN	CARBS	NUMBER OF MEALS	
WED					SUGAR ◯YES ◯NO
					COFFEE ◯YES ◯NO
					WATER ◯YES ◯NO
					WORKOUT◯YES ◯NO

	FATS	PROTEIN	CARBS	NUMBER OF MEALS	
THU					SUGAR ◯YES ◯NO
					COFFEE ◯YES ◯NO
					WATER ◯YES ◯NO
					WORKOUT◯YES ◯NO

	FATS	PROTEIN	CARBS	NUMBER OF MEALS	
FRI					SUGAR ◯YES ◯NO
					COFFEE ◯YES ◯NO
					WATER ◯YES ◯NO
					WORKOUT◯YES ◯NO

NOTES & ACCOMPLISHMENT

SAT	FATS	PROTEIN	CARBS	NUMBER OF MEALS	SUGAR ○ YES ○ NO
					COFFEE ○ YES ○ NO
					WATER ○ YES ○ NO
					WORKOUT ○ YES ○ NO

SUN	FATS	PROTEIN	CARBS	NUMBER OF MEALS	SUGAR ○ YES ○ NO
					COFFEE ○ YES ○ NO
					WATER ○ YES ○ NO
					WORKOUT ○ YES ○ NO

ENERGY LEVEL

	SUN	MON	TUE	WED	THU	FRI	SAT

OBSERVATIONS - HOW I FEEL

MY GOAL THIS WEEK

MEASUREMENT:

WEIGHT:

CHEST..............................WAIST...............................HIPS...................

DATA:		KETO DIET				

	FATS	PROTEIN	CARBS	NUMBER OF MEALS		
MON					SUGAR ◯YES ◯NO	
					COFFEE ◯YES ◯NO	
					WATER ◯YES ◯NO	
					WORKOUT ◯YES ◯NO	

	FATS	PROTEIN	CARBS	NUMBER OF MEALS		
TUE					SUGAR ◯YES ◯NO	
					COFFEE ◯YES ◯NO	
					WATER ◯YES ◯NO	
					WORKOUT ◯YES ◯NO	

	FATS	PROTEIN	CARBS	NUMBER OF MEALS		
WED					SUGAR ◯YES ◯NO	
					COFFEE ◯YES ◯NO	
					WATER ◯YES ◯NO	
					WORKOUT ◯YES ◯NO	

	FATS	PROTEIN	CARBS	NUMBER OF MEALS		
THU					SUGAR ◯YES ◯NO	
					COFFEE ◯YES ◯NO	
					WATER ◯YES ◯NO	
					WORKOUT ◯YES ◯NO	

	FATS	PROTEIN	CARBS	NUMBER OF MEALS		
FRI					SUGAR ◯YES ◯NO	
					COFFEE ◯YES ◯NO	
					WATER ◯YES ◯NO	
					WORKOUT ◯YES ◯NO	

NOTES & ACCOMPLISHMENT

SAT	FATS	PROTEIN	CARBS	NUMBER OF MEALS	SUGAR ◯ YES ◯ NO
					COFFEE ◯ YES ◯ NO
					WATER ◯ YES ◯ NO
					WORKOUT ◯ YES ◯ NO

SUN	FATS	PROTEIN	CARBS	NUMBER OF MEALS	SUGAR ◯ YES ◯ NO
					COFFEE ◯ YES ◯ NO
					WATER ◯ YES ◯ NO
					WORKOUT ◯ YES ◯ NO

ENERGY LEVEL

SUN	MON	TUE	WED	THU	FRI	SAT

OBSERVATIONS - HOW I FEEL

MY GOAL THIS WEEK

MEASUREMENT:

WEIGHT:

CHEST.............................WAIST................................HIPS.........................

DATA:		**KETO DIET**				

MON

FATS	PROTEIN	CARBS	NUMBER OF MEALS

SUGAR ◯ YES ◯ NO
COFFEE ◯ YES ◯ NO
WATER ◯ YES ◯ NO
WORKOUT ◯ YES ◯ NO

TUE

FATS	PROTEIN	CARBS	NUMBER OF MEALS

SUGAR ◯ YES ◯ NO
COFFEE ◯ YES ◯ NO
WATER ◯ YES ◯ NO
WORKOUT ◯ YES ◯ NO

WED

FATS	PROTEIN	CARBS	NUMBER OF MEALS

SUGAR ◯ YES ◯ NO
COFFEE ◯ YES ◯ NO
WATER ◯ YES ◯ NO
WORKOUT ◯ YES ◯ NO

THU

FATS	PROTEIN	CARBS	NUMBER OF MEALS

SUGAR ◯ YES ◯ NO
COFFEE ◯ YES ◯ NO
WATER ◯ YES ◯ NO
WORKOUT ◯ YES ◯ NO

FRI

FATS	PROTEIN	CARBS	NUMBER OF MEALS

SUGAR ◯ YES ◯ NO
COFFEE ◯ YES ◯ NO
WATER ◯ YES ◯ NO
WORKOUT ◯ YES ◯ NO

NOTES & ACCOMPLISHMENT

DATA:		KETO DIET				

SAT	FATS	PROTEIN	CARBS	NUMBER OF MEALS		
					SUGAR ○ YES ○ NO	
					COFFEE ○ YES ○ NO	
					WATER ○ YES ○ NO	
					WORKOUT ○ YES ○ NO	

SUN	FATS	PROTEIN	CARBS	NUMBER OF MEALS		
					SUGAR ○ YES ○ NO	
					COFFEE ○ YES ○ NO	
					WATER ○ YES ○ NO	
					WORKOUT ○ YES ○ NO	

ENERGY LEVEL

	SUN	MON	TUE	WED	THU	FRI	SAT

OBSERVATIONS - HOW I FEEL

MY GOAL THIS WEEK

MEASUREMENT:	WEIGHT:
CHEST............................WAIST...........................HIPS.........................	

DATA:			KETO DIET			

MON	FATS	PROTEIN	CARBS	NUMBER OF MEALS	SUGAR ○ YES ○ NO
					COFFEE ○ YES ○ NO
					WATER ○ YES ○ NO
					WORKOUT ○ YES ○ NO

TUE	FATS	PROTEIN	CARBS	NUMBER OF MEALS	SUGAR ○ YES ○ NO
					COFFEE ○ YES ○ NO
					WATER ○ YES ○ NO
					WORKOUT ○ YES ○ NO

WED	FATS	PROTEIN	CARBS	NUMBER OF MEALS	SUGAR ○ YES ○ NO
					COFFEE ○ YES ○ NO
					WATER ○ YES ○ NO
					WORKOUT ○ YES ○ NO

THU	FATS	PROTEIN	CARBS	NUMBER OF MEALS	SUGAR ○ YES ○ NO
					COFFEE ○ YES ○ NO
					WATER ○ YES ○ NO
					WORKOUT ○ YES ○ NO

FRI	FATS	PROTEIN	CARBS	NUMBER OF MEALS	SUGAR ○ YES ○ NO
					COFFEE ○ YES ○ NO
					WATER ○ YES ○ NO
					WORKOUT ○ YES ○ NO

NOTES & ACCOMPLISHMENT

DATA: _____   **KETO DIET**

SAT	FATS	PROTEIN	CARBS	NUMBER OF MEALS		
					SUGAR ○ YES ○ NO	
					COFFEE ○ YES ○ NO	
					WATER ○ YES ○ NO	
					WORKOUT ○ YES ○ NO	

SUN	FATS	PROTEIN	CARBS	NUMBER OF MEALS		
					SUGAR ○ YES ○ NO	
					COFFEE ○ YES ○ NO	
					WATER ○ YES ○ NO	
					WORKOUT ○ YES ○ NO	

ENERGY LEVEL

	SUN	MON	TUE	WED	THU	FRI	SAT

OBSERVATIONS - HOW I FEEL

MY GOAL THIS WEEK

MEASUREMENT:

CHEST.................................WAIST.................................HIPS.................................

WEIGHT:

....

DATA: _____ **KETO DIET**

	FATS	PROTEIN	CARBS	NUMBER OF MEALS		
MON					SUGAR ○ YES ○ NO COFFEE ○ YES ○ NO WATER ○ YES ○ NO WORKOUT ○ YES ○ NO	
TUE					SUGAR ○ YES ○ NO COFFEE ○ YES ○ NO WATER ○ YES ○ NO WORKOUT ○ YES ○ NO	
WED					SUGAR ○ YES ○ NO COFFEE ○ YES ○ NO WATER ○ YES ○ NO WORKOUT ○ YES ○ NO	
THU					SUGAR ○ YES ○ NO COFFEE ○ YES ○ NO WATER ○ YES ○ NO WORKOUT ○ YES ○ NO	
FRI					SUGAR ○ YES ○ NO COFFEE ○ YES ○ NO WATER ○ YES ○ NO WORKOUT ○ YES ○ NO	

NOTES & ACCOMPLISHMENT

SAT	FATS	PROTEIN	CARBS	NUMBER OF MEALS		
					SUGAR ○ YES ○ NO	
					COFFEE ○ YES ○ NO	
					WATER ○ YES ○ NO	
					WORKOUT ○ YES ○ NO	

SUN	FATS	PROTEIN	CARBS	NUMBER OF MEALS		
					SUGAR ○ YES ○ NO	
					COFFEE ○ YES ○ NO	
					WATER ○ YES ○ NO	
					WORKOUT ○ YES ○ NO	

ENERGY LEVEL

SUN	MON	TUE	WED	THU	FRI	SAT

OBSERVATIONS - HOW I FEEL

MY GOAL THIS WEEK

MEASUREMENT:

WEIGHT:

CHEST................................WAIST................................HIPS................................

DATA:		KETO DIET				

	FATS	PROTEIN	CARBS	NUMBER OF MEALS	SUGAR ○ YES ○ NO
MON					COFFEE ○ YES ○ NO
					WATER ○ YES ○ NO
					WORKOUT ○ YES ○ NO

	FATS	PROTEIN	CARBS	NUMBER OF MEALS	SUGAR ○ YES ○ NO
TUE					COFFEE ○ YES ○ NO
					WATER ○ YES ○ NO
					WORKOUT ○ YES ○ NO

	FATS	PROTEIN	CARBS	NUMBER OF MEALS	SUGAR ○ YES ○ NO
WED					COFFEE ○ YES ○ NO
					WATER ○ YES ○ NO
					WORKOUT ○ YES ○ NO

	FATS	PROTEIN	CARBS	NUMBER OF MEALS	SUGAR ○ YES ○ NO
THU					COFFEE ○ YES ○ NO
					WATER ○ YES ○ NO
					WORKOUT ○ YES ○ NO

	FATS	PROTEIN	CARBS	NUMBER OF MEALS	SUGAR ○ YES ○ NO
FRI					COFFEE ○ YES ○ NO
					WATER ○ YES ○ NO
					WORKOUT ○ YES ○ NO

NOTES & ACCOMPLISHMENT

DATA: _____ **KETO DIET**

SAT

	FATS	PROTEIN	CARBS	NUMBER OF MEALS		
					SUGAR ○ YES ○ NO	
					COFFEE ○ YES ○ NO	
					WATER ○ YES ○ NO	
					WORKOUT ○ YES ○ NO	

SUN

	FATS	PROTEIN	CARBS	NUMBER OF MEALS		
					SUGAR ○ YES ○ NO	
					COFFEE ○ YES ○ NO	
					WATER ○ YES ○ NO	
					WORKOUT ○ YES ○ NO	

ENERGY LEVEL

SUN	MON	TUE	WED	THU	FRI	SAT

OBSERVATIONS - HOW I FEEL

MY GOAL THIS WEEK

MEASUREMENT:

CHEST.................................WAIST.................................HIPS.................................

WEIGHT:

DATA:		**KETO DIET**				

	FATS	PROTEIN	CARBS	NUMBER OF MEALS	
MON					SUGAR ○ YES ○ NO
					COFFEE ○ YES ○ NO
					WATER ○ YES ○ NO
					WORKOUT ○ YES ○ NO
TUE	FATS	PROTEIN	CARBS	NUMBER OF MEALS	SUGAR ○ YES ○ NO
					COFFEE ○ YES ○ NO
					WATER ○ YES ○ NO
					WORKOUT ○ YES ○ NO
WED	FATS	PROTEIN	CARBS	NUMBER OF MEALS	SUGAR ○ YES ○ NO
					COFFEE ○ YES ○ NO
					WATER ○ YES ○ NO
					WORKOUT ○ YES ○ NO
THU	FATS	PROTEIN	CARBS	NUMBER OF MEALS	SUGAR ○ YES ○ NO
					COFFEE ○ YES ○ NO
					WATER ○ YES ○ NO
					WORKOUT ○ YES ○ NO
FRI	FATS	PROTEIN	CARBS	NUMBER OF MEALS	SUGAR ○ YES ○ NO
					COFFEE ○ YES ○ NO
					WATER ○ YES ○ NO
					WORKOUT ○ YES ○ NO

NOTES & ACCOMPLISHMENT

DATA:		KETO DIET					

SAT	FATS	PROTEIN	CARBS	NUMBER OF MEALS	SUGAR ◯ YES ◯ NO
					COFFEE ◯ YES ◯ NO
					WATER ◯ YES ◯ NO
					WORKOUT ◯ YES ◯ NO

SUN	FATS	PROTEIN	CARBS	NUMBER OF MEALS	SUGAR ◯ YES ◯ NO
					COFFEE ◯ YES ◯ NO
					WATER ◯ YES ◯ NO
					WORKOUT ◯ YES ◯ NO

ENERGY LEVEL

SUN	MON	TUE	WED	THU	FRI	SAT

OBSERVATIONS - HOW I FEEL

MY GOAL THIS WEEK

MEASUREMENT:

CHEST..................................WAIST..................................HIPS..................................

WEIGHT:

| DATA: _____ | KETO DIET | | | | |

	FATS	PROTEIN	CARBS	NUMBER OF MEALS	
MON					SUGAR ◯ YES ◯ NO
					COFFEE ◯ YES ◯ NO
					WATER ◯ YES ◯ NO
					WORKOUT ◯ YES ◯ NO
TUE					SUGAR ◯ YES ◯ NO
					COFFEE ◯ YES ◯ NO
					WATER ◯ YES ◯ NO
					WORKOUT ◯ YES ◯ NO
WED					SUGAR ◯ YES ◯ NO
					COFFEE ◯ YES ◯ NO
					WATER ◯ YES ◯ NO
					WORKOUT ◯ YES ◯ NO
THU					SUGAR ◯ YES ◯ NO
					COFFEE ◯ YES ◯ NO
					WATER ◯ YES ◯ NO
					WORKOUT ◯ YES ◯ NO
FRI					SUGAR ◯ YES ◯ NO
					COFFEE ◯ YES ◯ NO
					WATER ◯ YES ◯ NO
					WORKOUT ◯ YES ◯ NO

NOTES & ACCOMPLISHMENT

DATA:		**KETO DIET**				

SAT

FATS	PROTEIN	CARBS	NUMBER OF MEALS	SUGAR ○ YES ○ NO
				COFFEE ○ YES ○ NO
				WATER ○ YES ○ NO
				WORKOUT ○ YES ○ NO

SUN

FATS	PROTEIN	CARBS	NUMBER OF MEALS	SUGAR ○ YES ○ NO
				COFFEE ○ YES ○ NO
				WATER ○ YES ○ NO
				WORKOUT ○ YES ○ NO

ENERGY LEVEL

SUN	MON	TUE	WED	THU	FRI	SAT

OBSERVATIONS - HOW I FEEL

MY GOAL THIS WEEK

MEASUREMENT:	WEIGHT:
CHEST................ WAIST................ HIPS................	....

DATA:			KETO DIET				

MON	FATS	PROTEIN	CARBS	NUMBER OF MEALS	SUGAR ○YES ○NO
					COFFEE ○YES ○NO
					WATER ○YES ○NO
					WORKOUT ○YES ○NO

TUE	FATS	PROTEIN	CARBS	NUMBER OF MEALS	SUGAR ○YES ○NO
					COFFEE ○YES ○NO
					WATER ○YES ○NO
					WORKOUT ○YES ○NO

WED	FATS	PROTEIN	CARBS	NUMBER OF MEALS	SUGAR ○YES ○NO
					COFFEE ○YES ○NO
					WATER ○YES ○NO
					WORKOUT ○YES ○NO

THU	FATS	PROTEIN	CARBS	NUMBER OF MEALS	SUGAR ○YES ○NO
					COFFEE ○YES ○NO
					WATER ○YES ○NO
					WORKOUT ○YES ○NO

FRI	FATS	PROTEIN	CARBS	NUMBER OF MEALS	SUGAR ○YES ○NO
					COFFEE ○YES ○NO
					WATER ○YES ○NO
					WORKOUT ○YES ○NO

NOTES & ACCOMPLISHMENT

DATA: _____	**KETO DIET**					

	FATS	PROTEIN	CARBS	NUMBER OF MEALS		
SAT					SUGAR ◯ YES ◯ NO	
					COFFEE ◯ YES ◯ NO	
					WATER ◯ YES ◯ NO	
					WORKOUT ◯ YES ◯ NO	
	FATS	PROTEIN	CARBS	NUMBER OF MEALS		
SUN					SUGAR ◯ YES ◯ NO	
					COFFEE ◯ YES ◯ NO	
					WATER ◯ YES ◯ NO	
					WORKOUT ◯ YES ◯ NO	

ENERGY LEVEL

SUN	MON	TUE	WED	THU	FRI	SAT

OBSERVATIONS - HOW I FEEL

MY GOAL THIS WEEK

MEASUREMENT:

CHEST.................................WAIST.................................HIPS.................................

WEIGHT:

DATA:		KETO DIET				

	FATS	PROTEIN	CARBS	NUMBER OF MEALS		
MON					SUGAR ◯ YES ◯ NO	
					COFFEE ◯ YES ◯ NO	
					WATER ◯ YES ◯ NO	
					WORKOUT ◯ YES ◯ NO	
TUE	FATS	PROTEIN	CARBS	NUMBER OF MEALS	SUGAR ◯ YES ◯ NO	
					COFFEE ◯ YES ◯ NO	
					WATER ◯ YES ◯ NO	
					WORKOUT ◯ YES ◯ NO	
WED	FATS	PROTEIN	CARBS	NUMBER OF MEALS	SUGAR ◯ YES ◯ NO	
					COFFEE ◯ YES ◯ NO	
					WATER ◯ YES ◯ NO	
					WORKOUT ◯ YES ◯ NO	
THU	FATS	PROTEIN	CARBS	NUMBER OF MEALS	SUGAR ◯ YES ◯ NO	
					COFFEE ◯ YES ◯ NO	
					WATER ◯ YES ◯ NO	
					WORKOUT ◯ YES ◯ NO	
FRI	FATS	PROTEIN	CARBS	NUMBER OF MEALS	SUGAR ◯ YES ◯ NO	
					COFFEE ◯ YES ◯ NO	
					WATER ◯ YES ◯ NO	
					WORKOUT ◯ YES ◯ NO	

NOTES & ACCOMPLISHMENT

DATA: _____ **KETO DIET**

	FATS	PROTEIN	CARBS	NUMBER OF MEALS			
SAT					SUGAR ◯ YES ◯ NO		
					COFFEE ◯ YES ◯ NO		
					WATER ◯ YES ◯ NO		
					WORKOUT ◯ YES ◯ NO		

	FATS	PROTEIN	CARBS	NUMBER OF MEALS			
SUN					SUGAR ◯ YES ◯ NO		
					COFFEE ◯ YES ◯ NO		
					WATER ◯ YES ◯ NO		
					WORKOUT ◯ YES ◯ NO		

ENERGY LEVEL

	SUN	MON	TUE	WED	THU	FRI	SAT

OBSERVATIONS - HOW I FEEL

MY GOAL THIS WEEK

MEASUREMENT:

WEIGHT:

CHEST............... WAIST............... HIPS...............

DATA:		KETO DIET				

MON	FATS	PROTEIN	CARBS	NUMBER OF MEALS	SUGAR ○YES ○NO
					COFFEE ○YES ○NO
					WATER ○YES ○NO
					WORKOUT ○YES ○NO

TUE	FATS	PROTEIN	CARBS	NUMBER OF MEALS	SUGAR ○YES ○NO
					COFFEE ○YES ○NO
					WATER ○YES ○NO
					WORKOUT ○YES ○NO

WED	FATS	PROTEIN	CARBS	NUMBER OF MEALS	SUGAR ○YES ○NO
					COFFEE ○YES ○NO
					WATER ○YES ○NO
					WORKOUT ○YES ○NO

THU	FATS	PROTEIN	CARBS	NUMBER OF MEALS	SUGAR ○YES ○NO
					COFFEE ○YES ○NO
					WATER ○YES ○NO
					WORKOUT ○YES ○NO

FRI	FATS	PROTEIN	CARBS	NUMBER OF MEALS	SUGAR ○YES ○NO
					COFFEE ○YES ○NO
					WATER ○YES ○NO
					WORKOUT ○YES ○NO

NOTES & ACCOMPLISHMENT

DATA: _____	**KETO DIET**					

SAT	FATS	PROTEIN	CARBS	NUMBER OF MEALS	SUGAR ○ YES ○ NO
					COFFEE ○ YES ○ NO
					WATER ○ YES ○ NO
					WORKOUT ○ YES ○ NO

SUN	FATS	PROTEIN	CARBS	NUMBER OF MEALS	SUGAR ○ YES ○ NO
					COFFEE ○ YES ○ NO
					WATER ○ YES ○ NO
					WORKOUT ○ YES ○ NO

ENERGY LEVEL

SUN	MON	TUE	WED	THU	FRI	SAT

OBSERVATIONS - HOW I FEEL

MY GOAL THIS WEEK

MEASUREMENT:

CHEST................................WAIST................................HIPS................................

WEIGHT:

DATA:		KETO DIET			

	FATS	PROTEIN	CARBS	NUMBER OF MEALS	
MON					SUGAR ◯ YES ◯ NO
					COFFEE ◯ YES ◯ NO
					WATER ◯ YES ◯ NO
					WORKOUT ◯ YES ◯ NO

	FATS	PROTEIN	CARBS	NUMBER OF MEALS	
TUE					SUGAR ◯ YES ◯ NO
					COFFEE ◯ YES ◯ NO
					WATER ◯ YES ◯ NO
					WORKOUT ◯ YES ◯ NO

	FATS	PROTEIN	CARBS	NUMBER OF MEALS	
WED					SUGAR ◯ YES ◯ NO
					COFFEE ◯ YES ◯ NO
					WATER ◯ YES ◯ NO
					WORKOUT ◯ YES ◯ NO

	FATS	PROTEIN	CARBS	NUMBER OF MEALS	
THU					SUGAR ◯ YES ◯ NO
					COFFEE ◯ YES ◯ NO
					WATER ◯ YES ◯ NO
					WORKOUT ◯ YES ◯ NO

	FATS	PROTEIN	CARBS	NUMBER OF MEALS	
FRI					SUGAR ◯ YES ◯ NO
					COFFEE ◯ YES ◯ NO
					WATER ◯ YES ◯ NO
					WORKOUT ◯ YES ◯ NO

NOTES & ACCOMPLISHMENT

KETO DIET

SAT	FATS	PROTEIN	CARBS	NUMBER OF MEALS	
					SUGAR ○ YES ○ NO
					COFFEE ○ YES ○ NO
					WATER ○ YES ○ NO
					WORKOUT ○ YES ○ NO

SUN	FATS	PROTEIN	CARBS	NUMBER OF MEALS	
					SUGAR ○ YES ○ NO
					COFFEE ○ YES ○ NO
					WATER ○ YES ○ NO
					WORKOUT ○ YES ○ NO

ENERGY LEVEL

	SUN	MON	TUE	WED	THU	FRI	SAT

OBSERVATIONS - HOW I FEEL

MY GOAL THIS WEEK

MEASUREMENT:

CHEST................................WAIST................................HIPS................................

WEIGHT:

DATA:		KETO DIET				

MON

FATS	PROTEIN	CARBS	NUMBER OF MEALS		
				SUGAR ◯ YES ◯ NO	
				COFFEE ◯ YES ◯ NO	
				WATER ◯ YES ◯ NO	
				WORKOUT ◯ YES ◯ NO	

TUE

FATS	PROTEIN	CARBS	NUMBER OF MEALS		
				SUGAR ◯ YES ◯ NO	
				COFFEE ◯ YES ◯ NO	
				WATER ◯ YES ◯ NO	
				WORKOUT ◯ YES ◯ NO	

WED

FATS	PROTEIN	CARBS	NUMBER OF MEALS		
				SUGAR ◯ YES ◯ NO	
				COFFEE ◯ YES ◯ NO	
				WATER ◯ YES ◯ NO	
				WORKOUT ◯ YES ◯ NO	

THU

FATS	PROTEIN	CARBS	NUMBER OF MEALS		
				SUGAR ◯ YES ◯ NO	
				COFFEE ◯ YES ◯ NO	
				WATER ◯ YES ◯ NO	
				WORKOUT ◯ YES ◯ NO	

FRI

FATS	PROTEIN	CARBS	NUMBER OF MEALS		
				SUGAR ◯ YES ◯ NO	
				COFFEE ◯ YES ◯ NO	
				WATER ◯ YES ◯ NO	
				WORKOUT ◯ YES ◯ NO	

NOTES & ACCOMPLISHMENT

	FATS	PROTEIN	CARBS	NUMBER OF MEALS		
SAT					SUGAR ◯ YES ◯ NO	
					COFFEE ◯ YES ◯ NO	
					WATER ◯ YES ◯ NO	
					WORKOUT ◯ YES ◯ NO	

	FATS	PROTEIN	CARBS	NUMBER OF MEALS	
SUN					SUGAR ◯ YES ◯ NO
					COFFEE ◯ YES ◯ NO
					WATER ◯ YES ◯ NO
					WORKOUT ◯ YES ◯ NO

ENERGY LEVEL

	SUN	MON	TUE	WED	THU	FRI	SAT

OBSERVATIONS - HOW I FEEL

MY GOAL THIS WEEK

MEASUREMENT: WEIGHT:

CHEST.................................WAIST.................................HIPS.................................

DATA:			KETO DIET		

	FATS	PROTEIN	CARBS	NUMBER OF MEALS	
MON					SUGAR ○ YES ○ NO COFFEE ○ YES ○ NO WATER ○ YES ○ NO WORKOUT ○ YES ○ NO
	FATS	PROTEIN	CARBS	NUMBER OF MEALS	
TUE					SUGAR ○ YES ○ NO COFFEE ○ YES ○ NO WATER ○ YES ○ NO WORKOUT ○ YES ○ NO
	FATS	PROTEIN	CARBS	NUMBER OF MEALS	
WED					SUGAR ○ YES ○ NO COFFEE ○ YES ○ NO WATER ○ YES ○ NO WORKOUT ○ YES ○ NO
	FATS	PROTEIN	CARBS	NUMBER OF MEALS	
THU					SUGAR ○ YES ○ NO COFFEE ○ YES ○ NO WATER ○ YES ○ NO WORKOUT ○ YES ○ NO
	FATS	PROTEIN	CARBS	NUMBER OF MEALS	
FRI					SUGAR ○ YES ○ NO COFFEE ○ YES ○ NO WATER ○ YES ○ NO WORKOUT ○ YES ○ NO

NOTES & ACCOMPLISHMENT

DATA: _____	**KETO DIET**					

SAT	FATS	PROTEIN	CARBS	NUMBER OF MEALS	SUGAR ○ YES ○ NO
					COFFEE ○ YES ○ NO
					WATER ○ YES ○ NO
					WORKOUT ○ YES ○ NO

SUN	FATS	PROTEIN	CARBS	NUMBER OF MEALS	SUGAR ○ YES ○ NO
					COFFEE ○ YES ○ NO
					WATER ○ YES ○ NO
					WORKOUT ○ YES ○ NO

ENERGY LEVEL

	SUN	MON	TUE	WED	THU	FRI	SAT

OBSERVATIONS - HOW I FEEL

MY GOAL THIS WEEK

MEASUREMENT:

CHEST................................WAIST................................HIPS................................

WEIGHT:

DATA:		KETO DIET			

	FATS	PROTEIN	CARBS	NUMBER OF MEALS	
MON					SUGAR ◯ YES ◯ NO
					COFFEE ◯ YES ◯ NO
					WATER ◯ YES ◯ NO
					WORKOUT ◯ YES ◯ NO

	FATS	PROTEIN	CARBS	NUMBER OF MEALS	
TUE					SUGAR ◯ YES ◯ NO
					COFFEE ◯ YES ◯ NO
					WATER ◯ YES ◯ NO
					WORKOUT ◯ YES ◯ NO

	FATS	PROTEIN	CARBS	NUMBER OF MEALS	
WED					SUGAR ◯ YES ◯ NO
					COFFEE ◯ YES ◯ NO
					WATER ◯ YES ◯ NO
					WORKOUT ◯ YES ◯ NO

	FATS	PROTEIN	CARBS	NUMBER OF MEALS	
THU					SUGAR ◯ YES ◯ NO
					COFFEE ◯ YES ◯ NO
					WATER ◯ YES ◯ NO
					WORKOUT ◯ YES ◯ NO

	FATS	PROTEIN	CARBS	NUMBER OF MEALS	
FRI					SUGAR ◯ YES ◯ NO
					COFFEE ◯ YES ◯ NO
					WATER ◯ YES ◯ NO
					WORKOUT ◯ YES ◯ NO

NOTES & ACCOMPLISHMENT

DATA:		KETO DIET				

SAT	FATS	PROTEIN	CARBS	NUMBER OF MEALS	SUGAR ○ YES ○ NO
					COFFEE ○ YES ○ NO
					WATER ○ YES ○ NO
					WORKOUT ○ YES ○ NO

SUN	FATS	PROTEIN	CARBS	NUMBER OF MEALS	SUGAR ○ YES ○ NO
					COFFEE ○ YES ○ NO
					WATER ○ YES ○ NO
					WORKOUT ○ YES ○ NO

ENERGY LEVEL

	SUN	MON	TUE	WED	THU	FRI	SAT

OBSERVATIONS - HOW I FEEL

MY GOAL THIS WEEK

MEASUREMENT:

CHEST................WAIST................HIPS................

WEIGHT:

DATA:		KETO DIET				

	FATS	PROTEIN	CARBS	NUMBER OF MEALS		
MON					SUGAR ○ YES ○ NO	
					COFFEE ○ YES ○ NO	
					WATER ○ YES ○ NO	
					WORKOUT ○ YES ○ NO	

	FATS	PROTEIN	CARBS	NUMBER OF MEALS		
TUE					SUGAR ○ YES ○ NO	
					COFFEE ○ YES ○ NO	
					WATER ○ YES ○ NO	
					WORKOUT ○ YES ○ NO	

	FATS	PROTEIN	CARBS	NUMBER OF MEALS		
WED					SUGAR ○ YES ○ NO	
					COFFEE ○ YES ○ NO	
					WATER ○ YES ○ NO	
					WORKOUT ○ YES ○ NO	

	FATS	PROTEIN	CARBS	NUMBER OF MEALS		
THU					SUGAR ○ YES ○ NO	
					COFFEE ○ YES ○ NO	
					WATER ○ YES ○ NO	
					WORKOUT ○ YES ○ NO	

	FATS	PROTEIN	CARBS	NUMBER OF MEALS		
FRI					SUGAR ○ YES ○ NO	
					COFFEE ○ YES ○ NO	
					WATER ○ YES ○ NO	
					WORKOUT ○ YES ○ NO	

NOTES & ACCOMPLISHMENT

	FATS	PROTEIN	CARBS	NUMBER OF MEALS			
SAT					SUGAR ⃝ YES ⃝ NO		
					COFFEE ⃝ YES ⃝ NO		
					WATER ⃝ YES ⃝ NO		
					WORKOUT ⃝ YES ⃝ NO		
	FATS	PROTEIN	CARBS	NUMBER OF MEALS			
SUN					SUGAR ⃝ YES ⃝ NO		
					COFFEE ⃝ YES ⃝ NO		
					WATER ⃝ YES ⃝ NO		
					WORKOUT ⃝ YES ⃝ NO		

ENERGY LEVEL

SUN	MON	TUE	WED	THU	FRI	SAT

OBSERVATIONS - HOW I FEEL

MY GOAL THIS WEEK

MEASUREMENT:

WEIGHT:

CHEST................................WAIST................................HIPS................................

DATA:		KETO DIET				

MON

FATS	PROTEIN	CARBS	NUMBER OF MEALS	SUGAR	⭘ YES ⭘ NO
				COFFEE	⭘ YES ⭘ NO
				WATER	⭘ YES ⭘ NO
				WORKOUT	⭘ YES ⭘ NO

TUE

FATS	PROTEIN	CARBS	NUMBER OF MEALS	SUGAR	⭘ YES ⭘ NO
				COFFEE	⭘ YES ⭘ NO
				WATER	⭘ YES ⭘ NO
				WORKOUT	⭘ YES ⭘ NO

WED

FATS	PROTEIN	CARBS	NUMBER OF MEALS	SUGAR	⭘ YES ⭘ NO
				COFFEE	⭘ YES ⭘ NO
				WATER	⭘ YES ⭘ NO
				WORKOUT	⭘ YES ⭘ NO

THU

FATS	PROTEIN	CARBS	NUMBER OF MEALS	SUGAR	⭘ YES ⭘ NO
				COFFEE	⭘ YES ⭘ NO
				WATER	⭘ YES ⭘ NO
				WORKOUT	⭘ YES ⭘ NO

FRI

FATS	PROTEIN	CARBS	NUMBER OF MEALS	SUGAR	⭘ YES ⭘ NO
				COFFEE	⭘ YES ⭘ NO
				WATER	⭘ YES ⭘ NO
				WORKOUT	⭘ YES ⭘ NO

NOTES & ACCOMPLISHMENT

DATA:	KETO DIET				

SAT

FATS	PROTEIN	CARBS	NUMBER OF MEALS

SUGAR	○ YES ○ NO
COFFEE	○ YES ○ NO
WATER	○ YES ○ NO
WORKOUT	○ YES ○ NO

SUN

FATS	PROTEIN	CARBS	NUMBER OF MEALS

SUGAR	○ YES ○ NO
COFFEE	○ YES ○ NO
WATER	○ YES ○ NO
WORKOUT	○ YES ○ NO

ENERGY LEVEL

	SUN	MON	TUE	WED	THU	FRI	SAT

OBSERVATIONS - HOW I FEEL

MY GOAL THIS WEEK

MEASUREMENT:

CHEST................................WAIST................................HIPS................................

WEIGHT:

| DATA: | | KETO DIET | | | | |

	FATS	PROTEIN	CARBS	NUMBER OF MEALS		
MON					SUGAR ◯ YES ◯ NO	
					COFFEE ◯ YES ◯ NO	
					WATER ◯ YES ◯ NO	
					WORKOUT ◯ YES ◯ NO	

	FATS	PROTEIN	CARBS	NUMBER OF MEALS	
TUE					SUGAR ◯ YES ◯ NO
					COFFEE ◯ YES ◯ NO
					WATER ◯ YES ◯ NO
					WORKOUT ◯ YES ◯ NO

	FATS	PROTEIN	CARBS	NUMBER OF MEALS	
WED					SUGAR ◯ YES ◯ NO
					COFFEE ◯ YES ◯ NO
					WATER ◯ YES ◯ NO
					WORKOUT ◯ YES ◯ NO

	FATS	PROTEIN	CARBS	NUMBER OF MEALS	
THU					SUGAR ◯ YES ◯ NO
					COFFEE ◯ YES ◯ NO
					WATER ◯ YES ◯ NO
					WORKOUT ◯ YES ◯ NO

	FATS	PROTEIN	CARBS	NUMBER OF MEALS	
FRI					SUGAR ◯ YES ◯ NO
					COFFEE ◯ YES ◯ NO
					WATER ◯ YES ◯ NO
					WORKOUT ◯ YES ◯ NO

NOTES & ACCOMPLISHMENT

DATA:		**KETO DIET**				

	FATS	PROTEIN	CARBS	NUMBER OF MEALS		
SAT					SUGAR ⭘ YES ⭘ NO	
					COFFEE ⭘ YES ⭘ NO	
					WATER ⭘ YES ⭘ NO	
					WORKOUT ⭘ YES ⭘ NO	

	FATS	PROTEIN	CARBS	NUMBER OF MEALS		
SUN					SUGAR ⭘ YES ⭘ NO	
					COFFEE ⭘ YES ⭘ NO	
					WATER ⭘ YES ⭘ NO	
					WORKOUT ⭘ YES ⭘ NO	

ENERGY LEVEL

😄 🙂 😏 😮 😣 😵

SUN	MON	TUE	WED	THU	FRI	SAT

OBSERVATIONS - HOW I FEEL

MY GOAL THIS WEEK

MEASUREMENT:

WEIGHT:

CHEST................................WAIST................................HIPS................................

DATA:		KETO DIET			

MON

FATS	PROTEIN	CARBS	NUMBER OF MEALS	SUGAR ○YES ○NO
				COFFEE ○YES ○NO
				WATER ○YES ○NO
				WORKOUT ○YES ○NO

TUE

FATS	PROTEIN	CARBS	NUMBER OF MEALS	SUGAR ○YES ○NO
				COFFEE ○YES ○NO
				WATER ○YES ○NO
				WORKOUT ○YES ○NO

WED

FATS	PROTEIN	CARBS	NUMBER OF MEALS	SUGAR ○YES ○NO
				COFFEE ○YES ○NO
				WATER ○YES ○NO
				WORKOUT ○YES ○NO

THU

FATS	PROTEIN	CARBS	NUMBER OF MEALS	SUGAR ○YES ○NO
				COFFEE ○YES ○NO
				WATER ○YES ○NO
				WORKOUT ○YES ○NO

FRI

FATS	PROTEIN	CARBS	NUMBER OF MEALS	SUGAR ○YES ○NO
				COFFEE ○YES ○NO
				WATER ○YES ○NO
				WORKOUT ○YES ○NO

NOTES & ACCOMPLISHMENT

| DATA: | | KETO DIET | | | | |

SAT

	FATS	PROTEIN	CARBS	NUMBER OF MEALS

SUGAR ⭘ YES ⭘ NO
COFFEE ⭘ YES ⭘ NO
WATER ⭘ YES ⭘ NO
WORKOUT ⭘ YES ⭘ NO

SUN

	FATS	PROTEIN	CARBS	NUMBER OF MEALS

SUGAR ⭘ YES ⭘ NO
COFFEE ⭘ YES ⭘ NO
WATER ⭘ YES ⭘ NO
WORKOUT ⭘ YES ⭘ NO

ENERGY LEVEL

SUN	MON	TUE	WED	THU	FRI	SAT

OBSERVATIONS - HOW I FEEL

MY GOAL THIS WEEK

MEASUREMENT:	WEIGHT:
CHEST........... WAIST............ HIPS...........	

DATA:		KETO DIET				

MON	FATS	PROTEIN	CARBS	NUMBER OF MEALS	SUGAR ⚪ YES ⚪ NO
					COFFEE ⚪ YES ⚪ NO
					WATER ⚪ YES ⚪ NO
					WORKOUT ⚪ YES ⚪ NO

TUE	FATS	PROTEIN	CARBS	NUMBER OF MEALS	SUGAR ⚪ YES ⚪ NO
					COFFEE ⚪ YES ⚪ NO
					WATER ⚪ YES ⚪ NO
					WORKOUT ⚪ YES ⚪ NO

WED	FATS	PROTEIN	CARBS	NUMBER OF MEALS	SUGAR ⚪ YES ⚪ NO
					COFFEE ⚪ YES ⚪ NO
					WATER ⚪ YES ⚪ NO
					WORKOUT ⚪ YES ⚪ NO

THU	FATS	PROTEIN	CARBS	NUMBER OF MEALS	SUGAR ⚪ YES ⚪ NO
					COFFEE ⚪ YES ⚪ NO
					WATER ⚪ YES ⚪ NO
					WORKOUT ⚪ YES ⚪ NO

FRI	FATS	PROTEIN	CARBS	NUMBER OF MEALS	SUGAR ⚪ YES ⚪ NO
					COFFEE ⚪ YES ⚪ NO
					WATER ⚪ YES ⚪ NO
					WORKOUT ⚪ YES ⚪ NO

NOTES & ACCOMPLISHMENT

	DATA:		KETO DIET		

DATA: _____   **KETO DIET**

SAT	FATS	PROTEIN	CARBS	NUMBER OF MEALS

	SUGAR	○ YES ○ NO
	COFFEE	○ YES ○ NO
	WATER	○ YES ○ NO
	WORKOUT	○ YES ○ NO

SUN	FATS	PROTEIN	CARBS	NUMBER OF MEALS

	SUGAR	○ YES ○ NO
	COFFEE	○ YES ○ NO
	WATER	○ YES ○ NO
	WORKOUT	○ YES ○ NO

ENERGY LEVEL

SUN	MON	TUE	WED	THU	FRI	SAT

OBSERVATIONS - HOW I FEEL

MY GOAL THIS WEEK

MEASUREMENT:

WEIGHT:

CHEST................................WAIST................................HIPS................................

DATA:		KETO DIET				

MON	FATS	PROTEIN	CARBS	NUMBER OF MEALS	SUGAR ◯ YES ◯ NO
					COFFEE ◯ YES ◯ NO
					WATER ◯ YES ◯ NO
					WORKOUT ◯ YES ◯ NO

TUE	FATS	PROTEIN	CARBS	NUMBER OF MEALS	SUGAR ◯ YES ◯ NO
					COFFEE ◯ YES ◯ NO
					WATER ◯ YES ◯ NO
					WORKOUT ◯ YES ◯ NO

WED	FATS	PROTEIN	CARBS	NUMBER OF MEALS	SUGAR ◯ YES ◯ NO
					COFFEE ◯ YES ◯ NO
					WATER ◯ YES ◯ NO
					WORKOUT ◯ YES ◯ NO

THU	FATS	PROTEIN	CARBS	NUMBER OF MEALS	SUGAR ◯ YES ◯ NO
					COFFEE ◯ YES ◯ NO
					WATER ◯ YES ◯ NO
					WORKOUT ◯ YES ◯ NO

FRI	FATS	PROTEIN	CARBS	NUMBER OF MEALS	SUGAR ◯ YES ◯ NO
					COFFEE ◯ YES ◯ NO
					WATER ◯ YES ◯ NO
					WORKOUT ◯ YES ◯ NO

NOTES & ACCOMPLISHMENT

DATA:		**KETO DIET**				

SAT

FATS	PROTEIN	CARBS	NUMBER OF MEALS	
				SUGAR ◯ YES ◯ NO
				COFFEE ◯ YES ◯ NO
				WATER ◯ YES ◯ NO
				WORKOUT ◯ YES ◯ NO

SUN

FATS	PROTEIN	CARBS	NUMBER OF MEALS	
				SUGAR ◯ YES ◯ NO
				COFFEE ◯ YES ◯ NO
				WATER ◯ YES ◯ NO
				WORKOUT ◯ YES ◯ NO

ENERGY LEVEL

SUN	MON	TUE	WED	THU	FRI	SAT

OBSERVATIONS - HOW I FEEL

MY GOAL THIS WEEK

MEASUREMENT:

CHEST.................................WAIST.................................HIPS.................................

WEIGHT:

DATA:		KETO DIET				

	FATS	PROTEIN	CARBS	NUMBER OF MEALS	SUGAR ○YES ○NO
MON					COFFEE ○YES ○NO
					WATER ○YES ○NO
					WORKOUT ○YES ○NO
	FATS	PROTEIN	CARBS	NUMBER OF MEALS	SUGAR ○YES ○NO
TUE					COFFEE ○YES ○NO
					WATER ○YES ○NO
					WORKOUT ○YES ○NO
	FATS	PROTEIN	CARBS	NUMBER OF MEALS	SUGAR ○YES ○NO
WED					COFFEE ○YES ○NO
					WATER ○YES ○NO
					WORKOUT ○YES ○NO
	FATS	PROTEIN	CARBS	NUMBER OF MEALS	SUGAR ○YES ○NO
THU					COFFEE ○YES ○NO
					WATER ○YES ○NO
					WORKOUT ○YES ○NO
	FATS	PROTEIN	CARBS	NUMBER OF MEALS	SUGAR ○YES ○NO
FRI					COFFEE ○YES ○NO
					WATER ○YES ○NO
					WORKOUT ○YES ○NO

NOTES & ACCOMPLISHMENT

DATA:		**KETO DIET**				

	FATS	PROTEIN	CARBS	NUMBER OF MEALS		
SAT					SUGAR ⭕ YES ⭕ NO	
					COFFEE ⭕ YES ⭕ NO	
					WATER ⭕ YES ⭕ NO	
					WORKOUT ⭕ YES ⭕ NO	

	FATS	PROTEIN	CARBS	NUMBER OF MEALS		
SUN					SUGAR ⭕ YES ⭕ NO	
					COFFEE ⭕ YES ⭕ NO	
					WATER ⭕ YES ⭕ NO	
					WORKOUT ⭕ YES ⭕ NO	

ENERGY LEVEL

SUN	MON	TUE	WED	THU	FRI	SAT

OBSERVATIONS - HOW I FEEL

MY GOAL THIS WEEK

MEASUREMENT:

WEIGHT:

CHEST................................WAIST..............................HIPS................

DATA:		KETO DIET				

MON

FATS	PROTEIN	CARBS	NUMBER OF MEALS		
				SUGAR ○ YES ○ NO	
				COFFEE ○ YES ○ NO	
				WATER ○ YES ○ NO	
				WORKOUT ○ YES ○ NO	

TUE

FATS	PROTEIN	CARBS	NUMBER OF MEALS		
				SUGAR ○ YES ○ NO	
				COFFEE ○ YES ○ NO	
				WATER ○ YES ○ NO	
				WORKOUT ○ YES ○ NO	

WED

FATS	PROTEIN	CARBS	NUMBER OF MEALS		
				SUGAR ○ YES ○ NO	
				COFFEE ○ YES ○ NO	
				WATER ○ YES ○ NO	
				WORKOUT ○ YES ○ NO	

THU

FATS	PROTEIN	CARBS	NUMBER OF MEALS		
				SUGAR ○ YES ○ NO	
				COFFEE ○ YES ○ NO	
				WATER ○ YES ○ NO	
				WORKOUT ○ YES ○ NO	

FRI

FATS	PROTEIN	CARBS	NUMBER OF MEALS		
				SUGAR ○ YES ○ NO	
				COFFEE ○ YES ○ NO	
				WATER ○ YES ○ NO	
				WORKOUT ○ YES ○ NO	

NOTES & ACCOMPLISHMENT

DATA:		KETO DIET				

SAT

FATS	PROTEIN	CARBS	NUMBER OF MEALS

SUGAR	◯ YES ◯ NO
COFFEE	◯ YES ◯ NO
WATER	◯ YES ◯ NO
WORKOUT	◯ YES ◯ NO

SUN

FATS	PROTEIN	CARBS	NUMBER OF MEALS

SUGAR	◯ YES ◯ NO
COFFEE	◯ YES ◯ NO
WATER	◯ YES ◯ NO
WORKOUT	◯ YES ◯ NO

ENERGY LEVEL

SUN	MON	TUE	WED	THU	FRI	SAT

OBSERVATIONS - HOW I FEEL

MY GOAL THIS WEEK

MEASUREMENT:

CHEST.................................WAIST...............................HIPS.......................

WEIGHT:

Made in United States
North Haven, CT
28 April 2022

18683065R00063